Healthy Eating for Life

Over 100 Simple and Tasty Recipes

Robin Ellis

Illustrated by Hope James

RIGHT
WAY

Constable & Robinson Ltd
55–56 Russell Square
London WC1B 4HP
www.constablerobinson.com

First published in the UK by Right Way,
an imprint of Constable & Robinson, 2014

Text copyright © Robin Ellis 2014
Illustrations copyright © Hope James 2014

The right of Robin Ellis to be identified as the author of this work has been
asserted by him in accordance with the Copyright, Designs & Patents Act 1988.

All rights reserved. This book is sold subject to the condition that it shall not, by
way of trade or otherwise, be lent, re-sold, hired out or otherwise circulated in any
form of binding or cover other than that in which it is published and without a
similar condition including this condition being imposed on the subsequent
purchaser.

A copy of the British Library Cataloguing in Publication Data
is available from the British Library

ISBN: 978-0-7160-2353-1 (paperback)
ISBN: 978-0-7160-2354-8 (ebook)

1 3 5 7 9 10 8 6 4 2

Printed and bound in the EU

Healthy
Eating
for Life

Bromley Libraries

30128 80135 582 0

About the Author

Robin Ellis is best known as having starred in the BBC classic serial, *Poldark*, playing Captain Ross Poldark. It is widely regarded as one of the most popular British costume dramas ever produced. Other TV and film appearances have included roles in *Fawlty Towers*, *Elizabeth R*, *Blue Remembered Hills*, *The Europeans* and *Heartbeat*. His most recent role was in the original Swedish version of the detective series *Wallander*.

In 1999 Robin was diagnosed with type 2 diabetes. Although he had no symptoms, he took the diagnosis seriously as his mother suffered with type 1 diabetes for 35 years. In the same year he and his wife, Meredith, moved to southwest France where he has become known locally as the 'Anglais' who cooks! By changing the way he ate and taking more exercise, Robin was able to control his blood sugar sufficiently to avoid taking medication for six years.

In 2011 Robin's collection of favourite dishes was published in *Delicious Dishes for Diabetics*. Now, in his second cookbook, Robin shows how anyone can easily enjoy the benefits of a healthy Mediterranean style of cooking.

Photos of many of his recipes and information about the workshops he runs can be found on Robin's blog at http://robin-ellis.net/

'That which one eats as the fruit of his
own labour is properly called food.'

Old proverb

Praise from Those Who Have Enjoyed Robin's Dishes

Carmen Callil, publisher and author:
'This is the kind of great book that teaches you how to cook as you go. Read, cook, eat and be healthy, a marvellous Mediterranean combination for happiness. Robin Ellis is a truly great cook. Here he is at his delicious best.'

Brian Cox, Scottish actor:
'Of course I am biased! Robin is a very old and dear friend! Even so, he is simply one the best cooks ever. Why? His cuisine is always a delicious culinary paradox, strong and delicate with an exquisite balance of flavours. One of the truly great treats of my life is a meal prepared by Robin – with the commitment, love and detail of a great actor preparing for a classical role. Once tasted, never forgotten!'

Donald Douglas, actor:
'His cooking is superb! Wonderful flavours, textures and presentation. His cookbook is a must for those who love their food, but also like to stay healthy!'

Lindsay Duncan, actress:
'Robin is the perfect cook to have as a friend. He loves food, cooks superbly and likes nothing more than sharing his food with as many people as he can get round a table. Generosity is at the heart of good cooking and Robin cooks to give pleasure. It always works.'

Louise Fletcher, Academy-Award winning actress (*One Flew Over the Cuckoo's Nest*):
'To have Sunday lunch at Robin's and to go home with his recipes is the perfect southwest France Sunday. Oh, let there be many more Sundays in the kitchen with Robin.

'Robin's cooking and Robin's recipes: simple, fresh and simply glorious.'

Romaine Hart, former cinema-owner (Screen on the Green/the Hill/ Baker Street):
'Robin's cooking did what five different medications failed to do: bring down my high blood pressure. I suffered a stroke and no medication brought my blood pressure below 177/70. After staying only one week with Robin and eating his delicious meals, it came down to 120/59.'

Sir Derek Jacobi, actor (Emmy, BAFTA, Olivier and Tony Awards):
'I can highly recommend Robin's delicious recipes, some of which I have had the pleasure of sampling at his table in France. The recipes have all the richness of classical Mediterranean cooking. Enjoy yourselves as I have with this mouth-watering cornucopia!'

Michael Pennington, actor and author:
'Robin Ellis has the gift of writing recipes that you can taste as you read them. Absolutely delicious.'

Eva Marie Saint, Hollywood legend, Academy-Award and Emmy winner:
'Robin Ellis is a superb chef! His cookbooks, filled with delicious and healthy recipes, have become my best friends in our kitchen.'

Imelda Staunton, actress:
'How can food this good – be this good for you!'

Timberlake Wertenbaker, playwright (*Our Country's Good*):
'I've used Robin's recipes again and again. They're elegant, delicious, imaginative and easy to use.

'The Basques are great cooks and giving a dinner in the Basque Country is scary. One also eats very late so no one wants anything too heavy. I always use one of Robin's recipes and end up with nothing but compliments and a demand for the recipe.

'"An English woman who can cook tuna!" someone said to me in complete astonishment. Of course, the recipe was Robin's.'

Contents

Appreciations

I want to thank Judith Mitchell, my editor at Constable and Robinson, for trusting me enough to do a second book and being such a positive and encouraging presence. She's a tennis fan and our rallies are always lively and enjoyable.

Hope James, whose drawings so enhanced *Delicious Dishes for Diabetics*, has done it again! Her illustrations, all sketched here, perfectly capture the spirit of this place, my kitchen and our everyday lives. Merci infiniment Hope!

Thanks to friends who kindly agreed to share their recipes for inclusion here. Tari Mandair, Romaine Hart, Conner Middleton-Whitney, Lina Abild-Jones, Hilton McRae, Helen Richmond, Charlotte Fraser, Julie Ide, Irv and Iris Molotsky and Janet Bradley.

Thanks too to my friends who have written such generous endorsements – please come and visit us again!

I could not have done this without the gentle hand of my wife Meredith Wheeler at my back. She is my taster-in-chief, my in-house inspiration – thumbs up or straight face, I know immediately from her reaction if a dish is a goer or a gonner! Does it have the 'ding' factor? That's the question at table. Thank you, Meredith, for your moral support, your tolerance of a sometimes moody cook, your judgement and above all for your love.

Introduction

'The easiest and most pleasurable way to eat *well* is to cook.'
(*New York Times*, 2013)

'No one is born a great cook, one learns by doing.'
(Julia Child, American cook, food writer and legend)

Eating healthily is an aspiration everyone can share – though it's not always easy to follow if the person believes that '*healthily*' is synonymous with '*tastelessly*'!

This person might bite the bullet, so to speak, adopt a diet, perhaps, to lose weight for a limited time, but revert to old habits when the target has been reached. Then the cycle begins again. Diets don't work in the long run.

The idea behind this book (and my earlier book *Delicious Dishes for Diabetics*) is to demonstrate that cooking these relatively simple recipes affords you a way of eating *healthily* that **can** be *tasty* – so tasty in fact that there's little temptation to return to the old habits.

Being willing to cook is a big help when making changes to the way one eats. (Julia Child admits she didn't start to cook until she was thirty-two – she just ate! Then there was no stopping her.) Even for those who aren't regular cooks, these recipes are easy to follow and an encouragement, I hope, to everyone to have a go – at cooking and eating them.

Healthy Eating for Life – a slow start

Meredith, my wife, spent her childhood in a northern suburb of Chicago. She remembers shocking her grandparents when they asked her where she'd like to go for her eleventh birthday dinner. '*McDonald's!*' she said firmly – head office in Chicago – the ever-expanding fast food chain. She, in turn, was disbelieving when I told her I had never been to McDonald's, never eaten a Big Mac or a cheese burger!

I grew up in 1950s London; for us convenience/fast food was fish and chips wrapped in newspaper with salt and a shake of the malt vinegar bottle – the smell of deep fried batter wafting over the stalls of the local Odeon or Regal cinema.

Those were the days. I was eating doughnuts oozing jam and cream and covered in sugar at morning break in school. Meredith was given sugar sandwiches – wedges of white bread with butter and white sugar as the filling – to help her recover from night-time attacks of croupe (a viral infection of the larynx, common in children). The austerity of the war years which left people hungry but, oddly, healthier was over.

It was time for treats – even Mr Powell, our kindly dentist in Putney, had a bowl of sweets on hand to help soothe nerves – and keep him in business!

That was more than half a century ago. We met in 1986… by which time we had both evolved/progressed towards healthier tastes.

Over the next decade I had the time to indulge my passion for cooking. I was working mainly as a voiceover actor in the sound studios around the Soho district of London. After sessions, I would shop in Berwick Street market and at nearby Italian delicatessens; then ride my old Raleigh boneshaker bike back home with a basket full of goodies and cook my heart out.

Our 'way of eating' was southern European/Mediterranean style – *La Cucina d'Italie* in the main – strong on olive oil, lots of vegetables, fruit, meat, fish and wine. Inspiration came from heroes like Elizabeth David, Marcella Hazan and Anna del Conte.

Social eating was sitting round our large pine table, with friends, in the expanded kitchen, which quickly established itself as the heart of the house.

For years Meredith and I ate reasonably healthily, we thought. So it came as a shock just before the millennium and six months after moving permanently to France to be told there was a good chance I was pre-diabetic.

Pre-diabetic?

Oh no! Surely not, I have no symptoms and I feel fine.

But I knew enough to realise that if it turned out to be true, lifestyle changes were on the cards.

My mother had died of a heart attack related to her thirty-year struggle with type 1 diabetes at the age of sixty-seven.

Change is always a challenge and in terms of eating habits hard to stomach, so to speak.

Why bother? It won't make any difference, like changing deckchairs on the Titanic. *We're all going to die anyway!*

When the diagnosis, type 2 diabetes, was confirmed and to help me dodge the problems my mother had faced, I had to make adjustments.

Out went the 'whites' – processed versions of everyday staples – white pasta, white rice, white bread. Instead wholewheat pasta, brown basmati rice, whole rye bread, became our staples and we now prefer them. (The glycemic index (GI) – explained on page 180 – helps as a guide.)

I say *we* because Meredith eats for the most part the way I do, though she is not diabetic.

It's surprising how quickly *dreaded change* can become the norm. We don't feel deprived – the changes we've made are relatively few and represent healthy choices for anyone.

Though for those with less immediate need – making changes may be more difficult. Not impossible though…

I'm reminded of a song in *My Fair Lady*, the musical version of Bernard Shaw's play *Pygmalion*. Henry Higgins, confirmed bachelor, speech therapist and general stick-in-the-mud, sings *I've grown accustomed to her face* in a state of ecstatic disbelief that cockney sparrow

Eliza Doolittle could capture his heart so completely. At the end of the song, he is not simply *resigned* to change, he's luxuriating in it.

Change is not only possible – it can even be preferable!

Healthy Eating for Life – not a prison sentence

'Healthy Eating for Life!' What's this?

Sounds like something handed down by a crusty old judge – a life sentence of eating humble pie for past sins.

'Prisoners at the bar, you have sinned most grievously, eating too much of the wrong stuff for too long. Bad habits must be punished! I therefore have no alternative but to sentence you to: HEALTHY EATING – FOR LIFE. Take them down.'

Ouch! But NO! Emphatically **No**!

This book is not promoting a diet of worms, grapefruit or any of the strict rule-ridden diets that are so guilt-inducing and hard to stick with.

It's a book for people who love good food and enjoy cooking it or at least are willing to try. All manner of food, cooked in all manner of ways, encompassing a balanced diet, avoiding extremes.

It is not a manual. I am not a nutritionist. If it teaches, it is only by example.

It favours eating in *a mindful manner* – a phrase for which I have to thank Meg Henkels. Meg was one of the brave pioneer attendees at my first cooking workshop. The description, like a tasty dish, hit the spot.

Cooking Empowers – and is the Key

When you cook you're in control of what you eat. The fact that I liked to cook helped me negotiate the early days after the diagnosis with more confidence; it would be more problematical for someone not able or not keen to cook.

Cooking is not a mystery only to be understood by the trained and ordained few, though many of the cooking shows on TV might lead you to think that.

There are exceptions, but so few of them are about encouraging us to get into the kitchen, break a few eggs and make omelettes.

These shows are mainly aired and viewed as light entertainment. Cooking as a contest, professional or amateur – the *turn-on* is the competition, not the cooking.

We can sit back and watch *them* do it – and then send out for a takeaway!

It's true some people hate to cook and there is not the same family cooking tradition in the Anglo–Saxon world as in the countries that border the Mediterranean, where even if the pressures of modern life threaten a break with the past and takeaways are taking over (McDonald's are popping up here like autumn mushrooms), 'Grandma's' cooking is firmly in the collective unconscious memory. Talking about food here in southwest France is as compulsive as talking about the weather and considered as legitimate a subject for serious conversation at dinner as politics or religion, and usually safer!

Cooking is a daily ritual for me, sometimes a chore, but more often a pleasure. One that involves shopping in our local markets – seeking out and buying produce from the same people each week, as the seasons pass; this is one of the delights of living here for me. Lining up the ingredients, preparing them for the pot, grill or oven; then carrying out the recipe. Step by step – it's an integral part of my everyday life.

Not everyone has the time I know, but simple food is not hard to cook and nor are the recipes in this book – that's the point.

Julia Child again:

'You don't have to cook fancy or complicated masterpieces – just good food from fresh ingredients'.

Try the Red Bean Chilli (page 88) for example – straightforward and explosive in taste. Or the Salmon Fillets Baked in Spinach (page 112) – elegant and quick to make.

If I can do it, anyone can.

The thing is to get started…

Go on – break a few eggs!

The Mediterranean Way

My first taste of the Mediterranean *way of eating* was an egg cooked in olive oil in Lloret del Mar on the Costa Brava in Spain in 1953. It went into the memory bank as a 'wow!' I was twelve and olive oil was only available in chemists in the UK, used essentially for medicinal purposes.

I quickly understood from many trips abroad in the following formative ten years that olive oil is the foundation of the way food is prepared in countries bordering the Mediterranean Sea, and that this way of cooking and eating reflects a way of life, albeit one that is in retreat from the forces of mass marketing and globalisation.

The basic values survive, though, and not only round the table.

Shops in Barcelona and Madrid close in the middle of the day as their owners take their long lunches and siestas. *La passeggiata* – the little stroll – still survives all over Italy as families enjoy an early evening amble before dinner, down the Via del Corso in Rome or round the Piazza del Campo in Siena. In our department in southwest France, the Prefect recently decreed that supermarkets stay closed on Sundays. There's still a sense that people are enough in control of their lives to take a break and reflect. To *live* mindfully in fact, as well as aspiring to eat that way!

Key Ingredients in the Mediterranean Way of Eating

The main elements of the Mediterranean way of eating are:

- Eating plenty of fresh fruit and vegetables
- Eating whole grains, brown rice, wholewheat pasta and legumes
- Seasoning food with herbs and spices (so less salt is required)
- Including nuts and seeds (dry roasting brings out the flavour)
- Reducing the amount of red meat in the diet
- Eating fish or shellfish at least twice a week
- Limiting dairy products (use low-fat versions)
- Cooking with olive oil rather than butter (I usually use extra virgin olive oil)

Don't forget to *taste* food as it cooks, to judge the seasoning and the doneness. *Sample* the simmering tomato sauce to see if it's concentrated enough. *Test* the green bean to see how much longer it must cook. *Bite on* the strand of spaghetti, to make sure it's done to your liking.

Be careful when handling fresh chillies as they can sting. Wash your hands thoroughly after handling them.

A pair of tongs is essential and a small wooden tasting spoon is nice too. I always use organic vegetable stock cubes in my recipes.

American readers should follow the cup measurements (see conversion chart on page 180) when measuring volumes of liquid since UK (not US) pints are used in the recipes.

Bon appétit – Buono apetito!

1
Soups

All the soups in this section are vegetarian, except for the Chicken Broth and the Smoky Cauliflower Soup, where I'm going to try substituting smoked paprika for the smoky bacon one of these days as an alternative.

There are surprising soups like Courgette/Zucchini, and Brussels Sprout, plus a silky Mushroom Soup that is really just, well, mushrooms!

My soup of the moment is Pasta e Ceci – winter comfort soup par excellence – seasonally matched by a Tuscan White Bean Soup. Both are substantial and warming, evoking steaming bowls by the fireside. Pumpkin Soup is another.

Chilled Curried Apple is a simple summer soup and a conversation starter: What soup is this?

Soup makes a tasty light supper – in keeping with the whole thrust of the book – to encourage healthy eating.

Pasta e Ceci (Pasta and Chickpea Soup)

Serves 4

This thick comforting soup has been eaten in Italy since Roman times. There are many variations but a constant flavour is rosemary.

450 g/1 lb cooked chickpeas – tinned or bottled
6 tbsp olive oil
1 carrot – chopped fine
1 stick of celery – chopped fine
1 small onion – peeled and chopped fine
4 garlic cloves – peeled and pulped in a mortar with 1 tsp of salt
pinch of cayenne pepper (optional)
a sprig each of rosemary and sage
1 tbsp tomato concentrate
750 ml/1½ pints vegetable stock
Parmesan rind (optional)
180 g/7 oz small tubular pasta
salt and black pepper
olive oil to swirl in each bowl

1. Purée two-thirds of the cooked chickpeas in a food mixer.
2. Heat the olive oil in a large pan and gently sauté the carrot, celery and onion until they soften – about 10 minutes.
3. Add the garlic, the cayenne if using, and the herbs, mixing them in for a couple of minutes.
4. Stir in the tomato concentrate and cook for a further couple of minutes. Stir in the chickpeas and the vegetable purée. Add the stock and the Parmesan rind if using and bring the soup gently to the boil. Add the pasta and stir well, making sure the purée doesn't stick to the bottom of the pan. Season and simmer until the pasta is done – adding more water if it gets too thick. Serve hot with swirls of your best olive oil.

Roast Red Pepper and Tomato Soup

Serves 4

On our way back from a book signing in Cornwall, we enjoyed a steaming bowl of tomato soup at a bistro in Totnes. It was so good I was inspired to make my own version when I got home.

800 g/1 lb 12 oz tomatoes – cut into large chunks
250 g/8 oz red peppers – deseeded and chopped into large chunks
1 medium onion – peeled and chopped into large chunks
3 garlic cloves – peeled and chopped
1 tbsp olive oil
salt and pepper
2 tsp cider vinegar
300 ml/10 fl oz vegetable stock – I used ½ an organic
   vegetable stock cube in hot water
fresh basil to serve
olive oil to swirl in each bowl

1. Preheat the oven to 230°C/450°F/Gas Mark 8. Cover a shallow oven tray with foil and brush it with olive oil.
2. Gather the tomatoes, peppers, onion and cloves in a bowl. Pour over the olive oil. Season with salt and pepper and mix well. Tip this mix onto the oven tray and spread it evenly. Put into the hot oven for 30 minutes. It should come out nicely singed.
3. Let it cool a little then tip it all into a food processor and whizz to a roughish finish. (I don't mind the bits of tomato and pepper skin, but you have the option of lifting these off after the cooling period.)
4. Add the cider vinegar and stock, stir well and reheat. Check the seasoning. Serve with a little fresh basil sprinkled on top and a swirl of olive oil.

Pumpkin Soup

Serves 2

This is easy. Perfect after a winter walk; just looking at the colour warms you up. It's adapted from a recipe in *Leaves from our Tuscan Kitchen*, which gives a peak into the day-to-day ways of cooking in a Tuscan villa in the late nineteenth century.

1 medium onion – peeled and chopped
450 g/1 lb pumpkin – chopped with its skin
2 tbsp olive oil
1 tsp coriander powder
½ tsp cumin powder
¼ tsp cayenne powder
salt and pepper
500 ml/1 generous pint stock

1. Put the onion and the pumpkin pieces in a saucepan with the olive oil. Add the spices and salt and pepper. Turn everything over, cover and sweat over a low heat for 20 minutes to soften the vegetables.

2. Add the stock and cook uncovered for a further 20 minutes until the pumpkin is tender enough to liquidise.

3. Liquidise the mix. This is best done with a stick mixer – it saves much washing up!

4. A pinch of chopped parsley is a nice touch in each bowl. I cut up some rye bread, a slice each, into crouton-size pieces, sauté in a little olive oil and add a pinch each of salt and cumin powder. You could dry roast some pumpkin seeds to sprinkle on the top. Meredith suggests that sautéed bacon bits would be good too.

Mushroom Soup

Serves 4

The meatiness of mushrooms makes them ideal for making soup. Not much else is needed – garlic, parsley with a sprinkling of nutmeg and seasoning. This is adapted from a recipe in Carolyn McCrum's very handy *The Soup Book*, published over 30 years ago. It's simple, quickly done and very tasty.

1 tbsp olive oil
450 g/1 lb mushrooms – wiped clean with a damp piece of
   kitchen paper and chopped roughly
1 garlic clove – chopped
2 tbsp parsley – chopped
½ tsp grated nutmeg
salt and pepper
1 litre/2 pints stock
pinch of chopped parsley for each bowl

1. Heat the oil in a large saucepan. Add the mushrooms and stir thoroughly – the oil will quickly be absorbed. Cook over a low heat until the mushrooms start to release their liquid.
2. Add the garlic, parsley and nutmeg. Season with pepper and a little salt.
3. Add the stock and bring to a simmer. Cook gently for 15 minutes.
4. Let it cool a little before liquidising and check the seasoning. Sprinkle each bowl with a pinch of parsley.

Tuscan White Bean Soup with Cabbage

Serves 4

An autumn/winter soup with a big *presence*. Adapted from Leslie Forbes' *A Table in Tuscany*.

7 tbsp olive oil plus olive oil to swirl in each bowl
2 sticks of celery and 2 carrots – chopped small
2 leeks – cleaned and chopped small
3 or 4 tinned tomatoes – chopped up with their liquid
1 large garlic clove – peeled and pulped
sprig of fresh thyme
1 whole green cabbage – quartered, stem removed and shredded
800 g/28 oz cooked white beans – canned or bottled or dried, soaked and cooked (see page 161) – drained but their liquid retained
500 ml/1 pint stock

1. Heat 6 tablespoons of the oil in a large saucepan. Sweat the celery, carrots and leeks until tender – about 20 minutes.
2. Mix in the tomatoes, garlic and thyme. Cook for 5 minutes. Add half the shredded cabbage, season with salt and pepper, and cook for 10 minutes.
3. Purée three-quarters of the beans in a mixer with a little of their liquid. Add the bean water, the bean purée and the remaining beans to the soup and stir. Cook for an hour, stirring it regularly to stop it sticking and burning. Add a little of the stock each time you stir. This is meant to be a thick soup; it's up to you how loose you make it, just be careful not to dilute the depth of taste. While the soup cooks, sauté the rest of the cabbage in the remaining tablespoon of olive oil to serve as a topping when you present the soup. Serve hot with swirls of your best olive oil.

Soups

Chicken Broth

Serves 6

A traditional remedy for winter chills.

'Please, just some broth today!' was the request that morning from the sick bed.

Meredith had been fighting the 'lurgy' since Christmas Day. Not a person to give in lightly to a tickle in the throat, she had been up and back to bed all week. Time for broth!

Put in a large pot:

1 chicken
1 carrot – chopped
2 sticks of celery – roughly chopped
outer parts of a fennel bulb – roughly chopped
1 onion – peeled and roughly chopped
1 small garlic bulb – with the top sliced off
3 bay leaves
couple of parsley sprigs
couple of slices fresh ginger
a few peppercorns
1.5 litres/3 pints vegetable stock

1. Heat slowly up to a simmer. Cover and leave to bubble for an hour and a half.
2. Carefully remove the chicken and set aside. Remove the cooked vegetables with a slotted spoon, add a cut-up **carrot**, half a cut-up **fennel bulb** and some **broccoli** and cook them until they soften.
3. Serve them with the broth and a little of the very tender chicken. The rest of the chicken can be used for salad or sandwiches, while the rest of the broth can be refrigerated overnight for the fat to rise, be skimmed off and the soup reheated.

Lentil Soup

Iris Molotsky, our indomitable hostess in Washington DC, introduced us to this satisfying lentil soup – adapted from a recipe by chef Joan Swensen of Swilly's in Pullman, WA – perfect for warming the cockles on chilly winter nights.

2 tbsp olive oil
1 medium onion – peeled and chopped fine
1 stick of celery – chopped fine
1 medium carrot – chopped fine
½ small green pepper – chopped fine
1 large fennel bulb – diced large
4 cloves of garlic – pulped in a mortar with a tsp of salt
2 tsp each of cumin powder and curry powder
¾ tsp allspice
1 tsp each of cinnamon powder and cayenne pepper
450 g/1 lb pale-green flat or Puy (grey-green) lentils
1 x 400 g/14 oz tin tomatoes – drained and broken up
1 litre/2 pints stock and 2 litres/4 pints water
salt and pepper
low-fat/no-fat yogurt – a dollop a bowl
fresh coriander or parsley – chopped

1. Heat the oil in a large casserole over a medium heat. Add the onion, celery, carrot, green pepper, fennel and garlic. Stir well and soften gently for 5 minutes.
2. Add the cumin, curry powder, allspice, cinnamon and cayenne pepper. Cook for a minute, stirring in the spices.
3. Stir in the lentils and tomatoes, and then add the stock and water. Bring to a simmer and cook uncovered for an hour.
4. Season with salt and pepper. Serve with a dollop of yogurt and a pinch of chopped coriander or parsley in each bowl.

Brussels Sprout Soup

Serves 4

I've always liked Brussels sprouts, which were on the winter menu in the 1950s. Clearly Ma knew not to overcook them and I have a memory of mushing them with the gravy from the Sunday roast. She added chestnuts to them at Christmas – even better! Preparing them for the pan was often my job on a Sunday morning. 'Cut across the base, peel away the outer leaves and make a cross' were the instructions. 'Why?' I asked. 'To make them cook more quickly.'

This delicious and surprising soup is quick to prepare and has a pleasing light green colour. It's not a thick soup but is nourishing on a winter night.

2 medium onions – peeled and chopped
450 g/1 lb Brussels sprouts – outer leaves removed, bottoms
    trimmed, sprouts cut in half
1 tbsp olive oil
1 tsp butter
750 ml/1½ pints stock
salt and pepper
½ tsp ground nutmeg
1 tsp low-fat yogurt or cream per serving

1. In a saucepan gently sweat the onions and sprouts in the oil and butter for about 10 minutes.
2. Add the stock and bring to a simmer. Simmer gently for 20 minutes – the sprouts need to soften.
3. Liquidise (a handheld food mixer comes in handy here) and check the seasoning. Season lightly with salt (remembering that the stock cube may have salt in it), plenty of pepper and the nutmeg.
4. Serve hot with low-fat yogurt (or cream if you dare!).

Simple Celery Soup

Serves 4

I'd been wondering about celery soup. I always enjoyed the taste and crunch of raw celery; it felt like taking a bite of good health. It often featured on a plate of cheese at home in the 1950s, cutting the richness of a slice of Cheddar, cleansing the palate. I'd never made celery soup though. How well would it work without the usual addition of potato to thicken it? I tried other vegetables such as leek and red onion but then settled for just a medium onion. And for added flavour – white pepper and nutmeg. Here's my recipe for the simplest of celery soups.

1 tbsp olive oil
450 g/1 lb celery – sliced thinly
1 medium onion – peeled and chopped
1 clove of garlic – chopped
750 ml/1½ pints stock
¼ tsp ground nutmeg
salt and white pepper
pinch of chopped parsley for each bowl

1. Heat the oil in a large saucepan. Add the celery, onion and garlic. Turn them all thoroughly in the oil. Sweat (don't brown) these gently for about 5 minutes, to soften them.
2. Add the stock and continue cooking, uncovered, until the vegetables are tender – about 15 minutes.
3. Liquidise the soup (a handheld stick liquidiser saves a lot of washing up).
4. Stir in the nutmeg and season with salt and white pepper. Dry roasted walnuts are a neat addition – powdered in a coffee grinder – and folded into the soup at the end. Serve each bowl with a pinch of parsley.

Smoky Cauliflower Soup

Serves 4

There is no potato, no cream and no cheese in this recipe adapted from one by Nigel Slater that I spotted in a newspaper; the key ingredient is smoked bacon. We had this for supper the other night and Meredith said, 'What is this? It's so creamy. It's not potatoes, is it? It's delicious.'

1 tbsp olive oil
50 g/2 oz smoked bacon – chopped
2 cloves of garlic – chopped
1 medium onion – peeled and chopped
1 large cauliflower
2 bay leaves
1 litre/2 pints stock
salt and pepper

1. Gently heat the oil in a pan and sauté the bacon bits until they colour a bit. Add the garlic and onion. Cook the mix for 5 minutes until the onion has softened.
2. Meanwhile, break up the cauliflower into florets and add to a large saucepan. When ready, add the onion and bacon mix to the cauliflower pan with the bay leaves and the stock. Cover and bring this mix up to a simmer and cook until the cauliflower is tender.
3. Lift a third of the mix out of the pan with a slotted spoon and into a bowl, letting the liquid fall back into the pan. Liquidise the contents of the pan and test the seasoning. Add the set-aside florets and serve the soup hot.

Ma's Gazpacho

Serves 4

It's a fair bet my mother first tasted this traditional summer soup from Andalusia in 1953 when my parents took my brother and me to the Costa Brava for a fortnight's holiday. Dad worked for British Railways and got a certain amount of concessionary travel in Europe. There were five hotels at that time in Lloret del Mar (five hundred plus now!). We stayed in one of them with a pretty courtyard, close to the beach.

1 kg/2 lb ripe tomatoes – chopped roughly, retaining their juice
½ large cucumber – peeled and diced
½ large red pepper – seeded and diced
2 spring onions/scallions – chopped
3 cloves of garlic – pulped in a mortar with 1 tsp salt
salt and pepper
3 tbsp red wine vinegar
2 tbsp olive oil
a few drops Tabasco (optional)
olive oil to swirl in each bowl
fresh basil (if you have it)

1. Put the first five ingredients in a food processor. Pulse them to a not too smooth finish. Empty this already tasty mix into a bowl and adjust the seasoning with salt and pepper.
2. Stir in the red wine vinegar and olive oil. Add a few drops of Tabasco (a matter of taste). Chill for a couple of hours or overnight.
3. A ladle each is enough – with a whirl of olive oil and a pinch of chopped fresh basil, to finish. I sometimes add an ice cube to each bowl.

Curried Leek Soup

Serves 4

This simple soup, made with a few leeks (in the fridge) and a mix of individual spices (on the shelf), is comforting and a good standby.

0.75 kg/1½ lb leeks – using mainly the white and pale green parts
25 g/1 oz butter
1 tbsp olive oil
½ tsp each of cumin, coriander, English mustard powder
    (substitute with a little more cayenne if you don't have it)
    and turmeric
pinch each of cinnamon, cayenne and salt
1 litre/2 pints stock
spoonful whisked yogurt to swirl in each bowl

1. Prepare the leeks by cutting away the damaged brown tops and trimming the root ends. To wash them effectively, cut them down centrally from the top to just above the root and then wash thoroughly to clear any muddy residue. Slice them finely.
2. Heat the butter and oil in a large saucepan. Add the sliced leeks (keep back a small handful for a garnish) and turn them over in the butter and oil. Sweat them gently for 5 minutes.
3. Sprinkle the spices over the leeks, mix them in and cook for a couple of minutes. Add the stock, bring it to the boil and simmer gently for 15 minutes.
4. Let the soup cool a little before liquidising into a smooth finish. Gently sauté the handful of leeks you kept back in a little oil or butter. Drop a small spoonful of whisked yogurt in each bowl, topped off with a pinch of the sautéed leeks.

Chilled Curried Apple Soup

Serves 4

This is adapted from the first *Riverford Farm Cookbook*. Refreshing in summer and warming, served hot, in winter, this soup gets the conversation going in company. We asked guests at lunch recently to guess what soup they thought it was – the puzzled faces said it all.

Turmeric, the brilliant yellow spice, has anti-inflammatory and antioxidant properties – important weapons in the battle to stay on top of diabetes. (Cumin, another spice in the soup, has these beneficial properties too.) Turmeric, which helps give this stunning summer soup its luminous colour, also has a gold medal ability to stain anything that comes into contact with it; so the rule is: handle with care – or rather with a spoon!

Which apples to use? I used Fuji last time, which are a favourite apple for me. Next time I'm going to try Granny Smith, an apple with a touch more tartness. You could also try a mix.

25 g/1 oz butter
1 medium onion – peeled and chopped
3 large apples – peeled, cored and chopped
½ tsp each of turmeric, cumin, coriander and English mustard
   powder (or you could whizz some seeds in a grinder or
   leave out)
¼ tsp cayenne pepper
¼ tsp cinnamon powder
500 ml/1 pint stock
salt and white pepper
juice of ½ lemon
crème fraîche or yogurt for garnish
mint leaves for garnish

1. Melt the butter in a pan. Add the onion and sauté gently to soften.
2. Add the apple pieces and the spices and mix in.
3. Add the stock, season with salt and pepper, and simmer gently for 15 minutes.
4. Liquidise to a smooth texture, using a food blender or hand mixer.
5. Let it cool before leaving in the fridge for a few hours or overnight.
6. A ladle and a half per bowl is perfect. Add the lemon juice and stir in before serving with a teaspoon of crème fraîche or yogurt and a mint leaf for garnish if you have it.

Courgette/Zucchini Soup

Serves 4

This is adapted from the River Café's recipe. It is simple and satisfying, with a light green hue and creamy texture – a welcome addition to the summer courgette/zucchini repertoire.

1 kg/2 lb courgettes/zucchini – as fresh as possible, washed
    and cut into 2.5-cm/1-inch pieces
2 cloves of garlic – chopped
2 tbsp olive oil
500 ml/1 pint stock
salt and pepper
50 g/2 oz grated Parmesan cheese – add more to your taste
1 small pot/125 g low-fat yogurt
a handful each of chopped parsley and chopped basil

1. Fry the courgettes and garlic in the oil until they are very tender and browned a little – about 30 minutes.
2. Add the stock and bring to a gentle simmer for 5 minutes.
3. Season with salt and pepper – taking care with the salt, assuming there is salt in the stock. Let the soup cool a little.
4. Remove a quarter of the courgette pieces and liquidise the rest with a food mixer or stick liquidiser. Stir in the cheese and yogurt, followed by the parsley and basil.
5. Reheat gently. Check the seasoning and bring up to a simmer.
6. Serve in warm bowls, with the reserved courgette pieces scattered on top.

2
Starters and Light Lunches

Lunch here is often an omelette made with two eggs and a sprinkling of Parmesan, accompanied by a green salad with some roasted pumpkin or sunflower seeds, fine slices of sweet onion and a simple dressing. Makes me hungry writing that!

Stuffed red/yellow pepper halves are another standby. The filling is mashed-up tuna made more interesting with chopped black olives and capers.

Shakshouka – difficult to say with your mouth full – is the lightly spiced Tunisian egg and pepper mix; delicious and new to me.

A plate of Percy's Peppers, topped with a poached egg and some tender green beans on the side would make a pretty picture and the perfect light lunch.

Celery au Gratin

Serves 2 as a main course, 4 as an accompanying vegetable

At the time of writing it's Oscar time of year, so categories are on my mind. Celery often features chez nous; sometimes in bit parts – literally – as one element of a soffritto, the finely chopped mixture of vegetables known as *mirepoix* in French, or in a supporting role as a dipping stick for sauces like anchoïade, hummus or guacamole. Here it comes out of the shadows and into the spotlight to take the lead, the eponymous role even, with a strong supporting cast. It can be assembled beforehand, overnight even, and popped in the oven shortly before you are ready to eat.

750 g/1½ lb celery (weigh after separating the sticks and
    discarding the damaged outer ones) – cut into short pieces
25 g/1 oz smoked bacon – as much fat as possible removed
    and chopped small
1 onion – peeled and chopped
2 cloves of garlic – chopped
1 tbsp olive oil
3 large tinned tomatoes – chopped
1 level tsp cayenne pepper
sprigs of thyme and a couple of bay leaves
salt
2 tbsp dry white wine
12 juicy black olives – stoned and halved
3 tbsp Parmesan cheese – grated

1. Steam the celery until it's tender and set aside. (Alternatively, simmer it in half a litre/1 pint of stock.)
2. Sauté the bacon, onion and garlic in the oil until they start to colour.
3. Add the chopped tomatoes with the cayenne pepper, herbs and a pinch of salt. Cook these gently for 5 minutes.
4. Add the wine and cook for another couple of minutes to let the wine evaporate.
5. Add the olives and cook for a couple of minutes.
6. Turn off the heat and add the celery, turning it over thoroughly in the sauce.
7. Heat the oven to 220°C/425°F/Gas Mark 7. Spread a layer of the celery mix over the base of an ovenproof gratin dish. Season and sprinkle over some Parmesan. Repeat the process – seasoning and sprinkling cheese over each layer. Finish with a layer of Parmesan. Place the dish on the highest shelf in the oven, checking it after 20 minutes. The gratin should come out sizzling with a pleasingly charred look. Let it rest for 15 minutes.

Melting Tomatoes with Rosemary and a Parmesan Topping

Serves 4

The combination of olive oil, rosemary, garlic and Parmesan is comforting and delicious. Served with a piece of wholewheat/rye toast, dribbled with olive oil, a poached egg and a simple salad, this makes an easy light lunch or supper.

2 cloves of garlic – peeled
2 stems of rosemary leaves – chopped fine
salt and pepper
2 tbsp olive oil
10 medium ripe tomatoes – cut in half
3 tbsp grated Parmesan cheese or more if needed

1. Preheat the oven to 200°C/400°F/Gas Mark 6. Put the garlic and rosemary together with a good pinch of salt and a few grindings of the peppermill in a mortar. Pulp the garlic and rosemary with the pestle. Add the olive oil and stir to make a rough paste.
2. Cover a shallow oven tray with foil and brush it with oil. Place the tomatoes on it cut-side up. Using a teaspoon, smooth a little of the garlicky paste on each half tomato.
3. Place the tray on the top rack of the oven and cook for about 20–30 minutes – the tomatoes should have softened and collapsed somewhat.
4. Take them out of the oven and place a small pile of Parmesan on each tomato half. Put the tray back in the oven for about 15 minutes, until the cheese has browned on top.

Aubergine/Eggplant Boats with Chermoula

Serves 4

Chermoula, the North African spice mix (page 63), is spread lightly over aubergine/eggplant halves. These are then baked in a moderately high oven until tender. There are nearly as many versions of chermoula as there are camels in the desert, so if you are short of one of the ingredients go ahead anyway; it just means there'll be another camel in the desert!

This recipe is based on one from Ottolenghi's cookbook *Jerusalem*. The thinner variety of aubergine works well for this. It makes a tasty starter or light lunch served with some dressed salad leaves and a small bowl of Baba Ganoush (see page 33).

4 thin aubergines/eggplants – halved carefully top to toe
salt

For the chermoula
2 tsp cumin powder and 2 tsp coriander powder
1 tsp smoked sweet paprika and 1 tsp cayenne powder
2 cloves of garlic – pulped in a mortar with a teaspoon of salt
2 tbsp parsley – chopped
rind of a preserved lemon – chopped fine
4 tbsp olive oil

1. Make a couple of diagonal slits each way in the flesh of the aubergines. Sprinkle with a little salt and leave to drain for an hour or so.
2. Preheat the oven to 200°C/400°F/Gas Mark 6. Put all the chermoula ingredients in a bowl and mix thoroughly.
3. Dry the aubergine halves. Spread a thinnish layer of the chermoula mix on each half. Bake in the oven for about 40 minutes, depending on the thickness of the aubergines.
4. Leave to cool a little.

Sweet Potato, Fennel and Smoky Bacon au Gratin

Serves 2-3

A meal–in–a–pot dish, inspired by a Nigel Slater recipe in a newspaper clipping I found recently.

2 tbsp olive oil
1 onion – peeled and chopped
2 sticks of celery – chopped
3 cloves of garlic – pulped with a teaspoon of salt
1 tsp rosemary leaves – chopped fine
50 g/2 oz smoked bacon – cubed
1 tsp smoked paprika
250 g/8 oz cooked chickpeas
1 medium sweet potato – peeled, sliced into thick rounds and these halved
1 fennel bulb – outer leaves removed, sliced thick on the vertical
280 ml/½ pint stock
200 ml/7 fl oz coconut cream
2 tbsp grated Parmesan cheese mixed with 2 tbsp breadcrumbs

1. Preheat the oven to 190°C/375°F/Gas Mark 5. Heat the oil in a medium size, shallow sauté pan. Fry the onion and celery for a couple of minutes over a medium heat.

2. Add the garlic, rosemary, bacon and paprika. Stir these together and continue cooking, stirring as the vegetables begin to soften and the bacon colours – about 10 minutes.

3. Turn the chickpeas into the pan and mix them in. Add the sweet potato half-rounds and the fennel slices, and mix them in. Ease in the stock and the coconut cream. Season with salt and pepper. Bring it to the boil and sprinkle over the Parmesan and breadcrumb mixture.

4. Place in the middle of the oven for about 30 minutes.

Baba Ganoush

Serves 4

I have fallen in love with Baba Ganoush! First there's the name – like a favourite childhood comforter. Then there's the smoky taste and the creamy texture. Spread thickly on toast with a green salad, it makes a perfect light lunch.

Aubergines/eggplants are singed on a burner for a smoky flavour and/or roasted in the oven; the flesh should be completely soft. It's then peeled. (You can leave out the burner bit; it just won't be so smoky.)

2 large aubergines/eggplants
3 tbsp tahini paste (usually available in jars at good grocery
    stores or healthfood shops)
2 cloves of garlic – peeled
juice of a lemon
2 tbsp olive oil (optional)
1 tsp salt

1. Make a couple of slits in the aubergines – to avoid explosions! Balance the aubergines, one after the other, on a low gas flame or under a medium grill, turning regularly to singe and soften them. The time it takes will depend on the size of the aubergine. They need to end up very soft.
2. Preheat the oven to 200°C/400°F/Gas Mark 6 if you choose to roast them. Put the aubergines onto a shallow oven tray and on the top shelf of the oven for 40 minutes or until they are collapsed and the flesh feels soft inside.
3. Let them cool down. Peel them carefully and transfer the flesh to a large bowl. Mix in the tahini, garlic, lemon juice, olive oil and salt, making a smoothish mash. Taste and add more salt, lemon juice and olive oil as needed.

Crunchy Broccoli, Garlic and Chilli with Lemon 'Thins'

Serves 4

This is adapted from an Ottolenghi recipe in his eponymous first cookbook. It has become the signal dish of his restaurants, he says. It's easy to understand why.

Tumble it over a small pile of salad leaves – radicchio, rocket, lettuce – dressed with olive oil, lemon juice and salt. It's a splendid starter.

450 g/1 lb broccoli – broken into bite-size pieces
2 tbsp olive oil
salt
4 tbsp olive oil
4 cloves of garlic – sliced as thin as you can
2 fresh red medium-hot chillies – deseeded and sliced
1 lemon – sliced very thin

1. Steam the broccoli – more than blanched, less than tender – still crunchy in other words.
2. Remove to a bowl and pour over 2 tablespoons of olive oil and season with salt.
3. Heat a grill pad to hot. Scatter the broccoli over it and let it char lightly. Return it to the serving bowl.
4. Heat the second batch of oil. When hot, cook the garlic and chilli slices until the garlic takes on some colour – this happens quickly so keep an eye on it!
5. Pour the mixture over the broccoli. Add the lemon slices and mix in carefully.
6. Serve on a bed of salad leaves of choice, dressed with olive oil, lemon juice and salt.

Percy's Peppers

Serves 4

Percy Piper picked a peck of pickled peppers.
A peck of pickled peppers Percy picked.
If Percy Piper picked a peck of pickled peppers,
Where's the peck of pickled peppers Percy Piper picked?

Of course, Peter is picking in the nursery rhyme but Percy is just as hard to say. Our friend Charlotte Fraser first served us this delicious dish of red peppers. The eponymous Percy is a friend of hers.

4 red peppers – cored, deseeded and sliced fine lengthways
3 or 4 cloves of garlic – peeled but left whole
2 tbsp olive oil – plus extra for dribbling
12 anchovy fillets – chopped
2 tbsp small capers
pepper to taste

1. In a large pan over a low heat, gently soften the peppers and the garlic cloves in the olive oil. It's worth taking the time to do this; undercooked peppers are as unpalatable as undercooked aubergines/eggplants. Take a strip of pepper out of the pan from time to time, to test for doneness.
2. In a small pan, melt the anchovies slowly in a little olive oil by stirring and mashing them. Add the capers to the melted anchovies and stir the mix into the peppers. Season with pepper.
3. Heat the oven to 180°C/350°F/Gas Mark 4. Turn the mixture into an ovenproof serving dish and pop it into the warm oven for 5 minutes, half an hour before you're ready to eat.

Spinach and Red Onion Frittata

Serves 4 as lunch, 6 as a starter

Frittata is an Italian omelette, made the opposite way to a French omelette. The 'trick' is in the time it takes. It's cooked over the lowest heat, for about 20 minutes; a French omelette is cooked over the highest heat, for less than a minute! The French version is fluffy, the Italian firm but not dry; more like a pastry-less quiche, served in slices. What they have in common, apart from eggs and cheese, is that you can fill them with pretty much what you fancy. Here I've chosen a mix of cooked spinach and sautéed red onion. Other options are: courgettes and onions; green beans; tomatoes; artichokes; plain cheese; or onions alone.

300 g/¾ lb spinach – washed and shaken free of water
salt and pepper
3 tbsp olive oil
1 medium red onion – peeled and sliced
6 eggs
50 g/2 oz Parmesan cheese – grated
½ tsp grated nutmeg

1. Put the spinach in a large saucepan on a low heat. There will be enough water clinging to the leaves to cook it down. Salt lightly as you put it in the pan. Let it melt down. Remove to a colander to drain and cool.

2. In a small frying pan, heat a tablespoon of the oil and sauté the onion gently until it caramelises some.

3. Squeeze the spinach free of water, without squeezing the life out of it! Loosen it up, separating it a little then turn it over with the onion and season with salt and pepper.

4. Break the eggs into a mixing bowl and whisk them. Fold in the spinach and onion mix and turn it all together thoroughly. Mix in the cheese and nutmeg. Season again lightly with salt and pepper.

5. Heat the remaining oil in a pan (25-cm/10-inch size). When it's hot add the mixture, spreading it evenly over the base. Turn the heat down to the lowest setting and let it cook for about 20 minutes on this very low heat. Use a heat diffuser if you think it is not low enough. Fifteen minutes into cooking turn on the grill. Test the top of the frittata. When there's only a small pool of the mix left on top, it is ready to go under the grill – briefly – to finish. It shouldn't take much more than a minute under the grill to come out a little browned on top.

Green Lentils with Chorizo and Smoked Paprika

Serves 4

A dish to see off the winter chill. This is adapted from a recipe by Australian cookery writer Jody Vassallo and is a relatively quick all-in-one dish for small company. It took me about 50 minutes from arriving back from the market to turning off the gas under the casserole. Chorizo – sausage of the moment – to be eaten in moderation of course!

If made earlier in the day, you may need extra water when reheating this dish, as the lentils will continue to absorb the liquid, but it shouldn't be swamped.

2 tbsp olive oil
2 chorizo sausages (I prefer spicy ones) – sliced into round chunks
50 g/2 oz pancetta or bacon – chopped
1 onion – peeled and chopped fine
1 carrot – chopped fine
1 stick of celery – chopped fine
1 small fennel bulb – outer casing and core removed, chopped into small chunks
1 tsp smoked paprika
120 ml/4 fl oz white wine
2 cloves of garlic – peeled and left whole
couple of bay leaves
250 g/8 oz green or Puy lentils (the small grey-green ones) – washed and drained
1 litre/2 pints water – with extra to hand
salt and pepper
small bunch of parsley – chopped

1. Heat the oil in a medium casserole and fry the sausage and pancetta or bacon until lightly coloured. Remove and set aside on a plate covered with kitchen paper to absorb the excess fat.
2. Add the onion, carrot, celery and fennel and cook these in the same sausage-informed oil for about 7 minutes, until they too are lightly coloured.
3. Return the sausage and bacon to the casserole, sprinkle over the smoked paprika, add the wine, garlic and bay leaves. When the wine has evaporated, add the lentils and the water. Bring up to a simmer, cover and cook until the lentils are tender – about 20–30 minutes.
4. Season well and serve in warm bowls with the parsley sprinkled over and perhaps a swirl of olive oil.

Shakshouka

Serves 2

A traditional North African favourite, this version is adapted from a recent discovery in Ottolenghi's sumptuous vegetable cookbook *Plenty*. The name means 'mixture' in Tunisian Arabic; it's better to stick to Shakshouka I reckon! It is often served in individual cast iron pans, which I imagine adds to the pleasure: *one pan and all for me!*

½ tsp cumin seeds – dry roasted in a medium pan
60 ml/2 fl oz olive oil
1 large red or yellow onion – peeled and sliced
2 red peppers – washed, deseeded and sliced thin
1 bay leaf, thyme leaves from a few sprigs, 2 tbsp parsley
3 large fresh ripe or tinned tomatoes – roughly chopped with
   the juices
60 ml/2 fl oz water
¼ tsp cayenne pepper and a pinch (few strands) saffron
salt and pepper
2 or 4 eggs

1. Dry roast the cumin seeds for a minute or two, taking care not to burn them.
2. Heat the oil in the pan over a medium heat and cook the onion for 5 minutes to soften it.
3. Add the peppers and the three herbs and turn everything over thoroughly. Cover the pan for 5 minutes to start the softening of the peppers. Cook a further 5 minutes uncovered.
4. Add the tomatoes, the water, a little at a time to avoid diluting the sauce, the two spices and season with salt and pepper. Cook for 15 minutes on a low heat, covering for a short time if you think the peppers need further softening. The result should be a lightly spicy sauce in which to poach the eggs.
5. Carefully break the eggs (2 or 4, your choice) into the sauce, leaving space between them. Cover the pan and cook, over a lowish heat, until the eggs are cooked to your taste.

Red Pepper Halves with Tuna Stuffing

Serves 4

This is a handy way to use up leftover rice. I tried it first with 100 per cent rye breadcrumbs instead of rice. It was good but rice lightens the stuffing.

Stuffing for 4 medium red pepper halves

1 x 200 g/7 oz tin/jar tuna – drained of oil/water and flaked with a fork
1 tbsp parsley – chopped
1 clove of garlic – peeled and chopped fine
1 tbsp capers – chopped
5 juicy black olives – stoned and chopped
3 tbsp Parmesan cheese – grated
4 tbsp *cooked* brown basmati rice
1 egg – beaten
salt and pepper
2 red peppers – halved carefully lengthwise and deseeded
2 tbsp wholewheat/rye breadcrumbs for sprinkling
olive oil
1 lemon – quartered

1. Heat the oven to 180°C/350°F/Gas Mark 4. Combine the first eight ingredients in a bowl and season well with salt and pepper. Check the taste and add more seasoning if necessary.

2. Lay the pepper halves on oiled foil in a shallow roasting tray and spoon the stuffing into them. Sprinkle with the breadcrumbs. Swirl olive oil generously over the peppers and put them in the middle of the oven. Cook for about 40 minutes, checking after 30 minutes that all's well. They should end up with some tasty charring, without being cindered! Serve with a lemon quarter each for squeezing.

3
Salads

A catchall word *salad* can include almost anything these days, except chocolate cake perhaps! If pressed for a preference, I'd say green leaves and/or summer vegetables are required. The ingredients of the Greek Salad on page 49 – simple, seasonal and very fresh – sum up the Mediterranean way of eating. It helps to be eating them with a view of the sea and a glass of Greek wine – retsina for me – but it's not essential. The traditional peasant Panzanella (overleaf) is a winner when tomatoes are at their ripest.

Panzanella - Tomato and Bread Salad

Serves 4

Rough country bread that's a couple of days old is best for this classic Italian summer salad. It's better to wait, too, until the tomatoes are ripe; their sweet juices will meld with the oil, vinegar and seasoning for the bread to soak up. You could also add black olives, anchovies, capers, tuna and mozzarella.

½ loaf of bread – crusts removed, torn into bite-size pieces
2 cloves of garlic – sliced wafer-thin
10 ripe tomatoes – peeled, quartered, the quarters halved and the juice saved
1 medium cucumber – peeled, quartered lengthways, seeded and diced
3 tbsp parsley – chopped
175 ml/6 fl oz olive oil
2 tbsp red wine vinegar
salt and pepper

1. Put the bread in a favourite bowl. Add the thinly sliced garlic. Add the cut-up tomatoes and their juice, the diced cucumber and the chopped parsley.
2. Make the dressing by whisking together the oil, vinegar, salt and pepper. Pour this over the salad and mix it in well but gently.
3. Leave it for an hour for everything to meld together.

Grilled Courgette/Zucchini, White Bean and Cherry Tomato Salad

Serves 2-3

This is based on a recipe in *Riverford Farm Cook Book*, with some rocket added. The sweeter the little tomatoes are, the better to contrast with the grilled/charred courgettes.

1 x 660 g/23 oz jar cooked cannellini (white beans) – rinsed
3 tbsp olive oil plus more to brush the courgettes and 1 tbsp
    to anoint the warmed beans
3 courgettes/zucchini – sliced into 0.5 cm (not too thick, not
    too thin) strips
a generous handful of ripe cherry tomatoes
a generous handful of basil leaves
1 clove of garlic – peeled and pulped in a mortar with a pinch
    of salt
salt
a handful of rocket

1. Heat the grill to hot. Put the beans in a small pan with a little water and warm them through over a low heat. Drain and moisten them with 1 tablespoon of olive oil. Add them to a bowl in which you will mix the salad.
2. Brush the courgettes/zucchini with oil and grill them on both sides until tender and nicely charred. Add them to the bowl.
3. Halve the cherry tomatoes and add them to the bowl.
4. Combine the basil, garlic, a pinch of salt and the 3 tablespoons of olive oil in a food mixer and whizz. Add this to the salad and turn it over carefully.
5. Lay the rocket in a wide bowl and gently empty the mixed salad into it and turn the salad again. Serve tepid or at room temperature.

Simple Rocket, Tomato and Goat's Cheese Salad

Serves 2-3

Rocket (arugula) is available everywhere these days. If you have the space, it's quick to grow – forty days from seed to plate – and a good source of vitamins A, B complex and C. We eat a lot of it! It makes an attractive base for this simple salad from Lombardy, spotted in Paola Gavin's *Italian Vegetarian Cooking*.

couple of handfuls of rocket leaves
½ red onion – peeled and sliced as thin as you can manage
2 largish tomatoes – not too thickly sliced
a few juicy black olives – de-stoned
a small goat's cheese – in smallish pieces

Dressing
1 tbsp red wine vinegar
3 tbsp olive oil
salt and pepper

1. Spread the rocket over the base of your favourite salad bowl. Add the onion. Follow with the tomatoes, olives and cheese.
2. Whisk the dressing ingredients together and pour the vinaigrette over the salad and toss just before eating.

Greek Salad

Tomatoes, cucumber (peeled or unpeeled), sweet (red) onion, black olives, feta cheese, olive oil, red wine vinegar, salt and pepper. A blue sky, a dry summer heat, a swimming pool or blue blue sea and a glass of retsina. The first nine ingredients are the essentials, the last five are preferable but not obligatory!

Red, pink, pale green, black and white are the colours looking up at you from the bowl on the table.

It works best if the tomatoes and cucumber are sun-ripe and juicy but the contrasting tastes of the feta, olives, olive oil, vinegar and seasoning make this national dish worth eating any time, anywhere.

In Greece, chunks, curls, slices and slabs lend a spirit of generosity to the brimming bowls presented. Chunks of tomato, curls of soft red onion, slices – thickish – of cucumber and slabs of feta; the last laid on top of the finished construction like small white tombstones.

The olives in Greece are the kalamata variety, similar to the small black olives that feature in that other summer wonder – Salade Niçoise. Their faint bitterness balances the sweetness of the tomatoes and cucumber. The juicy black *Olives Greques* from our market are a meaty alternative.

Add the dressing, turn the contents over and your fork will start jabbing in – involuntarily.

'Kali Orexi!'

'Buon appetito!'

'Bon appétit!'

Roasted Aubergine/Eggplant Slices with Feta and a Mint Vinaigrette

Serves 4

This is inspired by a recipe in Diana Henry's *Crazy Water Pickled Lemons*, a book with an unusual title and wonderful recipes. You could grill the aubergine slices, which gives them a slightly smoky taste, instead of using the oven.

2 large aubergines/eggplants – cut crossways or lengthways
    into thickish slices (2 cm/¾ inch), lightly salted and left for
    an hour to drain through a sieve or colander
olive oil for brushing the foil and the aubergines
salt and pepper
a small slab of feta cheese to crumble on top of the salad
    (optional)

Vinaigrette
1 tsp white wine or cider vinegar
1 tbsp balsamic vinegar
2 cloves of garlic – peeled and pulped with a little salt
2 tbsp olive oil
a large handful of mint leaves – roughly chopped

1. Heat the oven to 240°C/475°F/Gas Mark 9. Lightly brush the aubergine slices – patted dry – with olive oil. Cover shallow oven trays (you may need two or to repeat the process) with foil. Brush the foil with oil to prevent the slices sticking. Spread the slices on the trays. Place the trays in the upper part of the oven for 10 minutes.

2. Take the trays out from the oven and turn the slices over. Return them to the oven for a further 10 minutes.

3. Make sure the aubergines are done by piercing the thickest part with the tip of a knife – underdone aubergine is inedible. Take them out of the oven and spread them on a serving plate.

4. Whisk the vinaigrette ingredients together and pour over the slices while they are still warm. Flake the feta (if using) over the top. Serve at room temperature – leaving a little time for the flavours to meld.

Green (Frisée Lettuce) Salad with Roquefort Cheese and Dry Roasted Walnuts

Serves 4 as a starter

A lovely traditional salad from southwest France. The Roquefort caves, where the famous sheep's cheeses are aged, are not far from us. One day we'll visit.

Walnuts are seriously healthy eating! Here the toasted walnuts are a wonderful foil to the richness of the cheese.

50 g/2 oz walnuts
1 large frisée lettuce
½ sweet onion – peeled and sliced
100 g/4 oz Roquefort cheese

Dressing
salt and pepper
1 tbsp red wine vinegar
3 tbsp olive oil
1 tsp walnut oil – if you have it

1. Crack open the walnuts and separate the nuts from the shells, taking care not to include any tooth-threatening piece of shell. Dry roast the nut pieces over a gentle flame in a small frying pan, until they colour and give off the lovely aroma associated with dry roasted nuts!
2. Wash and spin-dry the salad leaves and add them to a large mixing bowl. Add the nuts and the onion slices.
3. Make the dressing: Put a pinch of salt in a small mixing bowl and mix in the vinegar. Add the two oils and whisk it all together. Add the cheese and spoon the vinaigrette over the salad. Turn it all over carefully and thoroughly.
4. Portion it out on small plates beforehand or pass the bowl round the table, allowing people to serve themselves.

Fennel and Orange Winter Salad

Serves 2

Seasonally crunchy, with a juicy orange and some sunflower seeds – putting one in mind of gentler seasons to come – this salad got the nod from Meredith at lunch the other day!

1 large fennel bulb – outer leaves removed and halved vertically, each cut half laid flat and sliced very thin
1 celery stalk – sliced thin
½ small sweet red onion – peeled and sliced thin
1 tbsp sunflower seeds – dry roasted in a frying pan on a low flame
1 tbsp parsley – chopped
a few shavings of Parmesan
1 juicy orange – carefully peeled (lifting off the white pith), halved and sliced thinly
salt for sprinkling
1 tbsp olive oil

1. Mix the first seven ingredients together with care in a favourite bowl.
2. Sprinkle with salt and the oil, adding more oil if you like. Lightly turn everything over. Check the seasoning and serve.

Radish, Spring Onion and Tuna Salad

Serves 2

I like radishes – the fresher, the better. They abound on the market stalls here at the beginning of May and look so inviting. There's a limit, though, to how many sharp little explosions in the mouth one can take – even if, as it's said, they are good for the digestion. What to do with them? I consulted Nancy Harmon Jenkins' book *The Mediterranean Diet Cookbook* and found the perfect lunch for a sunny May bank holiday. A green salad and a slice of goat's cheese round off this simple dish.

450 g/1 lb radishes – washed, trimmed and sliced any which way that suits (grating some into the bowl for a pretty picture)

juice of ½ lemon

1 tsp salt

2–3 tbsp parsley – chopped fine

2 sticks of celery – diced fine

2–3 spring onions/scallions, mainly the white part – chopped fine

100 g/4 oz jar of good tuna in olive oil – drained and forked into flakes

10–12 juicy black olives – stoned and halved

3 tbsp best olive oil you have

1. Mix the radishes with the lemon juice and salt in a bowl. Add the parsley, diced celery and spring onions. Add the tuna flakes. Sprinkle over the olives and the olive oil.
2. Admire the beauty of it for a moment – before turning it over carefully but thoroughly.

Quinoa Salad with Red Onion and Herbs

Serves 4

The streaks of red onion and the greens of the herbs laced through the off-white of the quinoa make an attractive-looking salad for all seasons.

150 g/6 oz quinoa (white, preferably, for the look)
340 ml/12 fl oz vegetable stock
1 tbsp olive oil
1½ tbsp freshly squeezed lemon juice
½ small red onion – sliced thin
1 small bunch each parsley and mint – chopped
salt and freshly ground black pepper

1. Place a saucepan over a low heat and pour in the quinoa. Let it dry roast for 5 minutes, stirring all the time.
2. Add the stock and bring to a simmer. Cover and cook for about 20 minutes until the quinoa has absorbed the liquid and is puffed up. Set aside to cool.
3. Add the oil and lemon juice to the cooled quinoa and stir in with a fork.
4. Fold in the red onion, mint and parsley, again stirring them in with a fork. Season to taste with salt and pepper.
5. Transfer the salad to a pretty plate. Sprinkle with some more mint and parsley.

Cucumber and Red Onion Salad

Serves 4 as a side salad

This can also serve as a relish for salmon – it depends on the volume.

1 large cucumber – peeled and sliced thin; a food mixer disc saves time here
1 small red onion – peeled and sliced thin
salt
1 tbsp cider vinegar
1 tsp Dijon mustard
pepper
1 tbsp parsley or dill – chopped

1. Combine the prepared cucumber and red onion and sprinkle with salt. Let the mix drain in a colander or sieve for 30 minutes or longer.
2. Spread the mix over a layer of kitchen paper, cover with a second layer and press down gently to lift off excess liquid. Put it on a favourite plate or in a bowl.
3. Whisk the vinegar and mustard together with some pepper and fold in the chopped dill or parsley. Pour this over the cucumber and onion and turn it all over.
4. Leave it to luxuriate in the mix for an hour in the fridge.

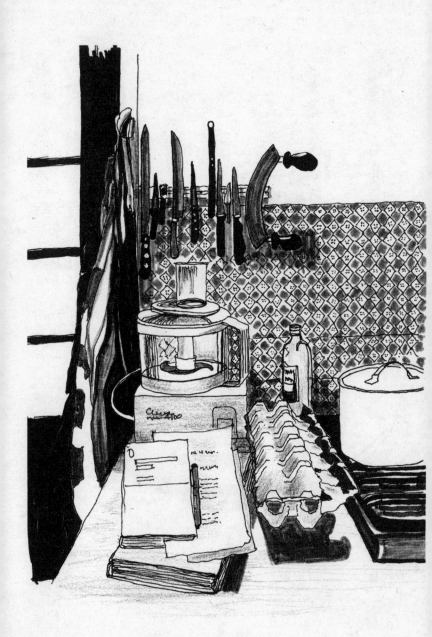

4

Dips and Sauces

Some sauces are for dipping too and some dips can serve as sauces, so I've combined them! 'Dips' often turn into scoops or even shovels; if they are tasty, they are moreish and if you aren't careful there's no room left for lunch. All four of these are good enough to qualify for the danger sign. Our friend Janet Bradley's different take on Guacamole (has 'Colorado' and 'Guacamole' ever been said in the same breath?) is one such – so approach it with caution! It's the small amount of mango that makes the difference.

Salad Dressing with Anchovies

This is a bold vinaigrette.

4 anchovy fillets – chopped
1 clove of garlic – peeled and pulped with a little salt in a
   mortar
turn of the pepper mill
2 tbsp red wine vinegar
4 tbsp olive oil
salt to taste – remembering the anchovies are salty

1. Add the chopped anchovy fillets to the garlic pulp in the mortar and meld them into a loose paste.
2. Add a little pepper. Mix in the vinegar then whisk in the oil.
3. Taste for salt and add extra if you think it needs it.

Quick Green Sauce

Serves 2-3

small bunch of parsley
1 clove of garlic – thinly sliced
1 tsp capers – chopped
salt – to taste
1 tbsp lemon juice
3 tbsp olive oil
1 tsp Dijon mustard

1. Make a pile of the first four ingredients. Chop through them until you have a dry version of the sauce. Put this reduced pile in a bowl, add the lemon juice and olive oil, and stir in the mustard.

Chimichurri (Argentine Parsley Sauce)

Serves 2-3

This is a new one on me. I like the name too, which can mean *made up of various ingredients in no particular order!* (There is a song from *Mary Poppins* that includes the words *Chim-chim cheree* – I doubt there's a connection though!) It makes a change from mint sauce with lamb and is good with grilled chicken and fish too. The first time I made it I didn't have fresh coriander, so I used double the amount of parsley.

1 clove of garlic – pulped in a mortar with 1 tsp salt
4 tbsp parsley – chopped
4 tbsp fresh coriander – chopped
a few grinds of the peppermill
2 tbsp chopped red onion
1 tbsp capers – rinsed
1 tbsp white wine/red wine/cider vinegar
3 tbsp olive oil

1. Put all the ingredients, except the olive oil, in a food processor and pulse it while slowly adding the oil.

Cumin Yogurt Sauce

Serves 4

Two neighbours came for supper the other night and I tried out a spicy chicken dish. It didn't impress Meredith, and our friends were polite but didn't exactly rave! I served a yogurt sauce with it, which I think *is* useful and tasty. I noticed Meredith tucking into it the next day with a fennel salad!

3 x 125 ml/4 fl oz pots no-fat organic yogurt
1 clove of garlic – peeled
½ tsp salt
1 tsp cumin powder
1 tbsp olive oil

1. Whisk the yogurt smooth – to make it a bit thicker, let it drain through a sieve into a bowl for half an hour or so.
2. Pulp the garlic in a pestle and mortar with the salt. Add the cumin and mix it in thoroughly. Fold in the olive oil.
3. Add this mix to the yogurt and whisk well in. Refrigerate until you are ready to eat.

Chermoula

A North African (Moroccan, Tunisian, Algerian) herb and spice mix used to marinade and flavour fish, fowl and vegetables. Try it with quail or chicken breasts. The aubergine/eggplant boats on page 31 are powered by a thin layer of it.

The measurements below are meant as a guide. Add a tablespoon of water or more to loosen the sauce if you need to.

2 tsp cumin powder
2 tsp coriander powder
1 tsp smoked sweet paprika
1 tsp cayenne powder
2 cloves of garlic – peeled and pulped with 1 tsp salt
rind of a preserved lemon – carefully removed and chopped fine
1 tsp grated fresh ginger
4 tbsp olive oil
1 handful each of flat-leaf parsley and fresh coriander

1. In a bowl, combine the first seven ingredients.
2. Gradually whisk in the olive oil until you have a smooth sauce.
3. Add the parsley and coriander and mix them in.

Quick Tomato Sauce

A handy standby sauce. It's wise to wear an apron and use a long wooden spoon for this.

2 tbsp olive oil
2 cloves of garlic – peeled and thinly sliced
2 sprigs rosemary – chopped
1 kg/2 lb fresh tomatoes – roughly chopped – or 2 large tins
   of tomatoes – drained of their juice and roughly chopped
salt and pepper

1. Heat the oil in a large pan and add the garlic and rosemary. Soften the garlic for a few seconds, being careful not to let it burn.
2. Add the tomatoes and cook over a high heat, stirring often, until the loose liquid has evaporated and little pockmarks appear on the surface. If you can part the red sea – running a spoon through it – it's done. Season with salt and pepper.

Pinzimonio

Pinzimonio, I discovered by a chance re-reading of Leslie Forbes' lovely book *A Table in Tuscany*, is a Tuscan olive oil dip, best made with the oil from newly harvested olives.

It can be served with raw or lightly cooked vegetables such as fennel, red and yellow peppers, celery, radishes and artichokes.

Simply pour some beautiful green olive oil on a plate, add a little sea salt and black pepper and dip a slice of vegetable into it.

Sometimes a little lemon juice is added – but this is frowned upon by Tuscans, according to Wilma Pezzini in her *Tuscan Cookbook*.

Meredith substituted rough country bread the other night for the vegetables and left out the salt and pepper – a parsimonious pinzimonio!

I watched in dismay from the stove area as Meredith and our two guests dipped and dipped – putting away helping after helping of this simple but moreish dish. 'You won't have any appetite left!'

Tarator

Serves 2

Tarata! Taraahh!

I've heard it described as a yogurt soup from Bulgaria and a sauce from Lebanon. My version is loose, lemony and lightly garlicky, to be enjoyed with meat or vegetables.

3 tbsp tahini
2 tbsp lemon juice
1 clove of garlic – peeled and pulped in a mortar with ½ tsp salt
⅓ tsp cumin powder
4 tbsp water
1 tbsp parsley – chopped
salt

1. Put the first five ingredients in a mixer and whizz to a smooth runny consistency. Stir in the chopped parsley, and add salt to your taste.

Molly's Smoked Mackerel Pâté

My mother Molly cooked for us every day on a small budget in the late 1940s and 1950s. She was resourceful and adventurous – not afraid to try new recipes inspired by trips abroad.

From her I learned that it was worth spending a little time in the kitchen – not least because I got to lick the bowls!

Her smoked mackerel pâté has a fair amount of melted butter in it, but the oily mackerel is a healthy counter to it. I like it best served on toasted rye bread. She wrote the recipe out for me on the back of an envelope and miraculously I still have it. Her flowing round hand is unmistakeable. Few of her written recipes survive, so I treasure this one.

2 smoked mackerel (about 450 g/1 lb)
150 g/6 oz unsalted butter
2 pinches cayenne pepper
2 pinches ground mace or nutmeg
2 tbsp lemon juice
freshly milled salt and black pepper
watercress sprigs for garnish
1 apple, sliced – to serve
lemon wedges – to serve

1. Remove the skins and bones from the fish and place in a food mixer.
2. Melt the butter but don't let it brown, and pour into the mixer and blend until smooth.
3. Turn the mixture into a bowl, work in the cayenne pepper, mace or nutmeg and lemon juice. Add salt and pepper, taste and add more if needed.
4. Pack into a mould and garnish with the watercress. The apple slices cut the richness of the pâté.

Hummus

This version has a bit of a kick to it. There's garlic, cumin and cayenne in this mix – with olive oil and lemon juice to loosen it.

250 g/8 oz cooked chickpeas – I prefer those in jars
3 cloves of garlic – peeled and chopped
½ tsp salt
3 tbsp tahini
1 tsp cumin powder
½ tsp cayenne pepper
2 tbsp olive oil
juice of 2 lemons

1. Put all the ingredients except the lemon juice in a food mixer and whizz smooth.
2. Add half the lemon juice and taste. Add the rest of the lemon juice as you like.

Janet's Colorado Guacamole

Serves 4-6

Our friend Janet Bradley passed this on – a Mexican 'wave' from the Rockies. She's a Coloradian artist and a neighbour. The mango is a nice twist on the conventional – but too much makes the dip too sweet.

3 medium avocados – halved and flesh scooped out
¼ small mango – peeled and chopped
2 cloves of garlic – peeled and pulped in a mortar with 1 tsp salt
juice of 2 limes
1 tsp cumin powder
1 tsp coriander powder
½ tsp chilli powder
1 jalapeño pepper – chopped fine
pepper and more salt if needed

1. Mash the avocado and mango flesh into a rough mush. Add the garlic and blend it in.
2. Stir in the lime juice, cumin, coriander and chilli.
3. Add the jalapeño pepper and taste for salt.
4. Serve with sticks of raw vegetables. Celery is a particularly good match.

5

Vegetables

It's Easter time as I write. Spring is doing her best to get established. Everyone is ready for a change on the vegetable stalls in the market. I bought half a kilo of asparagus, a couple of bunches of bright red radishes and some fleurs de broccoli, but the new season will take a few weeks to get going. I shall roast the asparagus at a high temperature with parboiled discs of sweet potato and some whole unpeeled garlic cloves, all seasoned well and turned in olive oil – an accompaniment to the rabbit with garlic and white beans (page 123) tonight. Roasting vegetables is popular at the moment – the rather alarmingly named *Blackened Brussels Sprouts* retain a lovely green succulence inside.

Smothered Broccoli

Serves 2-4

Poor broccoli is often the butt of jokes – probably because people remember it from their schooldays, served up looking limp and tasting of very little. These days the tendency is perhaps to undercook vegetables. Not this time! Italian cookery writer, Anna del Conte, first ate this unusual dish in a friend's house in Milan. In this recipe the broccoli is cooked longer than usual – covered – on a low heat. The flavours meld wonderfully and it becomes meltingly soft. Not a great looker, but a winner for taste!

2 tbsp olive oil
5 cloves of garlic – peeled, halved lengthways and the little
  green shoot removed
1 hot red chilli – sliced
700 g/1½ lb broccoli – the bunched florets broken up into
  bite-size pieces and the stalks stripped of their rough outer
  layer and diced
salt and pepper
1 lemon – quartered

1. Heat the oil in a sauté pan that has a tight-fitting cover. Add the garlic and chilli and fry for a couple of minutes.
2. Add the broccoli stalks and florets. Turn them over thoroughly in the oil. Cover the pan and turn the heat down to the lowest possible. Cook for 40 minutes – checking from time to time to prevent burning but taking care not to break up the softening broccoli into a mush!
3. Season with salt and pepper. A little lemon squeezed over makes a good finish.

Green Beans with Garlic, Red Chilli and Black Mustard Seeds

Serves 4

These have been a favourite for years. They go well with spicy food and make an effective complement – nice colour contrast as well – to a simply cooked salmon fillet. The recipe is adapted from one in Madhur Jaffrey's BBC cookbook *Indian Cookery*.

450 g/1 lb green beans – topped
4 tbsp olive oil
1 tbsp black mustard seeds
4 cloves of garlic – chopped very fine
1 dried red chilli – chopped fine
1 tsp salt
pepper

1. Cook the beans to just tender in plenty of lightly salted, boiling water. The fresher the beans, the quicker they cook. After 5 minutes, use tongs to whip one out of the water to test for doneness – test in this manner until you judge them ready. Plunge them into a bowl of cold water to stop them cooking further.

2. When you are ready to continue cooking, heat the oil in a frying pan and add the mustard seeds. When they start to pop, add the garlic. Cook until it starts to turn light brown – be careful not to burn it; it won't take long. Add the chilli and stir. Add the beans and the salt.

3. Turn the heat to low and fold the beans over in the oil and spices. (You are heating through and infusing the beans with the flavours; 2–3 minutes should do it.) Add the pepper.

Brussels Sprouts Sautéed with Parmesan and Breadcrumbs

Serves 2-3

This vegetable is controversial, often occasioning pursed lips. Those school meals to blame again, I suspect, for overcooking them to mush.

Sprouts like a good frost is one of the few gardening mantras I remember from growing up in the 1950s. My father must have said it. Dad grew vegetables, mainly root vegetables in winter but sprouts as well – on their extraordinary rods. Late autumn/winter is their season; the time of the first frosts. My mother would add the traditional chestnuts or bacon to liven them up. She didn't overcook them either.

This is a simple alternative, adapted from the wonderful *Leaves from our Tuscan Kitchen*.

450 g/1 lb Brussels sprouts – outer layers removed and larger
  ones halved
2 tbsp olive oil
2 tbsp Parmesan – grated
2 tbsp wholewheat breadcrumbs
salt and pepper

1. Steam the sprouts for about 10 minutes, to soften them but taking care not to overdo it. Remove from the heat.
2. Heat the oil in a sauté pan and when it's hot carefully transfer the sprouts to the pan. Sauté on a high heat until they show signs of browning.
3. Add the cheese and breadcrumbs and stir fry for a couple of minutes, scraping the breadcrumb and cheese mix off the base of the pan (they become deliciously crunchy), while turning the sprouts. Season with salt and pepper.

Blackened Brussels Sprouts

Serves 4 as a side vegetable

Iris Molotsky, our host on a recent trip to Washington DC and a fine cook herself, gave me this simple recipe. The results are surprising. Scorched black on the outside, they retain a lovely green succulence on the inside. They are all the rage it seems.

450 g/1 lb Brussels sprouts – outer parts trimmed
3 tbsp olive oil
salt and pepper

1. Preheat the oven to 200°C/400°F/Gas Mark 6. Place the sprouts in a bowl and add the olive oil, salt and pepper. Turn over to allow the oil to coat the sprouts thoroughly.
2. Empty them onto an oiled sheet of foil, spread over a shallow oven tray. Place the tray on the middle shelf of the oven. Roast for 30–45 minutes, depending on their size, shaking the pan every 10 minutes to brown them evenly. Reduce the heat if necessary to prevent them burning. They should be dark brown, almost black, when done but with a tender green interior.
3. Adjust the seasoning if necessary. Serve immediately.

Interesting Cabbage

Serves 2

A cabbage once got the job of representing my head. In 1971 I played the foolish, arrogant, headstrong Earl of Essex in *Elizabeth R* opposite a formidable Glenda Jackson as Elizabeth. The young jackanapes got it into his head to start a rebellion against the Virgin Queen. He'd been her favourite for years and had been forgiven much but this she couldn't ignore. He found himself on Tower Green with a rendezvous with the headsman.

The powers that be at BBC Television Centre decided the most realistic way to replicate the sound of a head being chopped off was to lop a cabbage in half! I have only recently been able to eat them without getting nervous! Here the abused cabbage is restored to its proper place – on the table.

2 tbsp olive oil
1 clove of garlic – sliced thinly
1 small onion – peeled and chopped small
1 small cabbage – halved vertically, cored and shredded thinly
10 juniper berries – squashed
salt and pepper

1. Heat the oil in a pan. When hot, sauté the garlic until it starts to colour. Add the onion and stir fry until the onion catches up with the garlic.
2. Add the cabbage and the juniper berries and turn all together thoroughly in the garlic, onion and oil mix. Cover the pan, lower the heat and cook for a further 10 minutes to soften the cabbage. Add a splash of water if the cabbage starts to catch. Be generous with the pepper and sprinkle some salt over.

Cauliflower Roasted with Garlic and Coriander Seeds

Serves 4 as a vegetable, 2 as a main course

I had bought three pretty little cauliflowers in the market and was looking for a new way to cook this seasonal beauty. The cauliflower falls into the 'What on earth am I going to do with it *this* time?' category of vegetables; like Swiss chard and fennel. A recipe in Delia Smith's *Winter Collection* gave me the idea for this.

I sprinkled some dry roasted sunflower seeds over the finished dish.

450 g/1 lb cauliflower – broken up into florets
1 generous tsp coriander seeds – pounded in a pestle and mortar
2 cloves of garlic – peeled and pulped with a small tsp of salt in a pestle and mortar
2 tbsp olive oil
salt and pepper

1. Preheat the oven to 200°C/400°F/Gas Mark 6. Put the cauliflower in a large bowl. Sprinkle over and mix in the crushed coriander seeds.

2. Whisk the crushed garlic and olive oil together. Mix in this little sauce, coating the florets thoroughly.

3. Spread them on oiled foil on a roasting tray in a single layer. Season with salt and pepper. Roast in the oven for about 30 minutes, checking for doneness after 20 minutes; they should be tender and charred a little.

4. If liked, dry roast some sunflower seeds in a pan on the hob and sprinkle them over the transformed cauliflower.

Roasted Chicory/Endive

Serves 2

In France they call the torpedo-like bulbs endive; in the UK it's chicory. *Vive la différence!*

This simple method is inspired by a recipe in an early Simon Hopkinson book, *Roast Chicken and Other Stories*. The bulbs are cooked in a low oven for two hours and emerge with 'Eat me!' written all over them.

Two medium endive *each* went well with roast chicken the other night, proving very popular: *'Encore! Encore!'*

2–3 tbsp olive oil
4 medium chicory/endive bulbs – outer leaves removed, bases
  sliced off and the bitter little cone carefully removed with
  the tip of a sharp knife
salt and pepper
juice of a lemon

1. Preheat the oven to 170°C/325°F/Gas Mark 3.
2. Heat the oil in a pan with a lid that can go in the oven. Place the bulbs in the pan and season with salt and pepper. To colour them, turn them in the oil over a medium-low flame. Add the lemon juice and let it bubble for a moment.
3. Cover the pan and put it in the oven for 2 hours. It's wise to check it now and again, adding a little water if necessary.

Green Beans with Ginger

Serves 4

I glory in green beans (*les haricots verts*), cooked just enough to be tender, yet still a vibrant green and not *too much* that they become flabby and dull in colour. As soon as the season starts here and the first piles appear in the markets, I'm looking for new ways to cook them.

I spotted this simple and surprising recipe in the *New York Times*. Armed with some new-season garlic and fresh-looking ginger, 'Give it a go!' I thought. This is my slightly adapted version which goes well with Butterflied Pork Chop (page 136).

2 cloves of new garlic – or the freshest looking you can find – peeled
a large thumbnail size piece of ginger – peeled and chopped small
1 tsp salt
450 g/1 lb green beans – topped, no need to tail
2 tbsp olive oil

1. Have a bowl of cold water ready to plunge the cooked beans into.
2. Pound the garlic, ginger and a teaspoon of salt into a pulp.
3. Bring a large saucepan of water to the boil. Add the beans and cook them until just tender to the bite; cooking tongs come in handy here to whip a bean out for a bite test. When you judge they're ready, transfer them quickly into the bowl of cold water, to stop them cooking further. Drain them and leave to dry a little.
4. Heat the olive oil in a large sauté pan. Add the beans, and the garlic and ginger gunge. Over a gentle heat, turn the beans in the mixture until they are nicely heated through. Taste them and add more salt if needed.

Pumpkin Roasted with Spices

Serves 2

The round red pumpkins that crowd the market stalls in winter are
works of art. Perfect spheres that stand upright, proudly showing off
their beauty. It seems a shame to cut them up and eat them – though
they still look a picture when in bits!

You can make a glowing soup with more or less the same
ingredients as below (see page 12).

Here the large dice are simply roasted for half an hour in a hottish
oven and spread on top of the Warm Lentil Salad (page 160) or eaten
as an accompanying vegetable.

1 small pumpkin – about 450 g/1 lb
1 tbsp olive oil
1 tsp cumin
½ tsp coriander
½ tsp cayenne pepper
salt and pepper

1. Preheat the oven to 220°C/425°F/Gas Mark 7.
2. There's no need to peel the skin of the pumpkin, just halve
   the pumpkin ball from top to bottom with a large knife and a
   great deal of care. Using a serving spoon, scoop out the
   seeds inside, leaving just the pumpkin flesh. Cut the two
   halves into bite-size bits and put them in a bowl.
3. Add the oil and the spices and season with salt and pepper.
   Turn the mix over thoroughly.
4. Spread it out over a shallow oven tray covered in foil (it saves
   scraping the charred bits off later). Roast for 30 minutes by
   which time the bits will have cooked through and charred a
   little. Serve as you like.

Peperonata

Serves 4

This is worth trying, as a vegetable or as a starter, just for the beauty of it! The perfect time for this is late summer when red and yellow peppers are piled high on the market stalls and the tomatoes are sweet end-of-season numbers. Serve for lunch on a piece of rye or wholewheat toast, with a poached egg on top.

A spoonful of tapenade (black olives and capers, see the recipe in *Delicious Dishes for Diabetics*) makes a nice contrast with the colours of Catalonia (to the south of us here – red and yellow) and cuts the sweetness of the peppers; but you have to make the tapenade!

1 tbsp olive oil
1 medium onion – peeled and sliced thinly
2 cloves of garlic – peeled and sliced
750 g/1½ lb red and yellow peppers (or red if you can'f find
    yellow) – deseeded and sliced in strips
2 bay leaves
350 g/12 oz ripe tomatoes – peeled and chopped
salt and pepper
1 tsp balsamic vinegar

1. Heat the oil in a medium pan you can cover. Add the onion and soften it for 5 minutes. Add the sliced garlic, turning it in the onion and oil and cook for a couple more minutes.
2. Add the pepper slices and the bay leaves, turning these over in the mixture. Cover the pan and cook for 15 minutes to soften the peppers, turning them a couple of times.
3. Add the tomatoes, some salt and pepper, mix them in and cover the pan again. Let this cook gently for 20 minutes. If the mix looks too liquid, cook it for another 5 minutes or so, uncovered. Add the balsamic vinegar and mix in well.

Tari's Stir-Fried Cabbage with Peas

Serves 4

Our friend Tari Mandair – the carefree cook from *Delicious Dishes* – was cooking lunch and I watched him stir-fry some cabbage to go with the chicken. Here's the recipe so you can replicate this beautifully green dish. Tari likes to cook this a little ahead of time to let the flavours meld, then he reheats it just before eating.

swirl of olive oil in the pan
1 tsp cumin seeds
1 medium cabbage – outer leaves removed, quartered, de-stemmed and sliced fine
1 tsp turmeric
pinch of red chilli flakes
couple of bay leaves
salt and pepper
couple of handfuls of frozen green peas

1. Heat the oil in a large sauté pan. Add the cumin seeds, and fry them briefly until they colour a little.
2. Add the cabbage, and turn it over thoroughly in the oil. Add the remaining spices and season with salt and pepper. Stir-fry the mix over a highish heat for about 5 minutes. The cabbage will wilt but retain a bit of a bite! Tari says that if the heat is too low, it will steam the cabbage and taste like hospital food and won't pick up the little charred flecks of brown that add to its deliciousness. But don't burn it!
3. Add the peas and turn them over with the cabbage.

6

Vegetarian Dishes

We are eating vegetarian meals more often than not in the evenings now. It seems to suit our digestive systems; seems to make sense. Some of these dishes are one-pot affairs, tempting me to call them convenience food – convenient in the sense that they can be assembled hours ahead and popped in the oven when a hard-working person gets home.

The soup, pasta, light lunches and pulses and grain sections have much to offer vegetarians too.

Aubergine/Eggplant Halves Topped with Tomato Sauce

Serves 2

These aubergine boats carry a different cargo from the ones in the Starter section (page 31) – a thickish tomato sauce.

2 aubergines/eggplants – halved lengthways
salt
olive oil
8 tbsp Quick Tomato Sauce (page 64)

1. Carefully, without piercing the skin, make two parallel diagonal slashes in the flesh side of the cut aubergines and repeat the process the other side, as though you were going to play noughts and crosses! Sprinkle with a little salt and leave to drain in a colander for an hour.
2. Preheat the oven to 200°C/400°F/Gas Mark 6.
3. Pat the four halves dry with kitchen paper. Brush with olive oil and place on a shallow oven tray covered with lightly oiled foil. Place on the middle shelf of the oven and cook until tender – about 40 minutes; the time depends on the size of the aubergines, but they must be soft.
4. Take them out of the oven and spread a couple of generous tablespoons of the tomato sauce on the top of each half – more if necessary. Return them to the oven for about 20 minutes. You can let them rest for 10 minutes before serving.

Courgette/Zucchini Gratin Italian Style

Serves 2 as a main course, 4 as a side dish

This is a classic Mediterranean dish and everyone has a way to do it.

3 good size courgettes/zucchini
1 tbsp olive oil
1 clove of garlic – chopped
salt and pepper
3–4 tbsp Parmesan cheese
Quick Tomato Sauce (page 64) – couple of tbsp for each layer

1. Prepare the courgettes: top and tail them, and slice them thinly. A food mixer does this nicely.
2. Heat the oil in a large saucepan. Add the sliced courgettes, the chopped garlic clove and ½ teaspoon of salt. Turn everything over several times to coat the vegetables lightly in the oil. Cook on a low heat until the courgettes are wilted. Set them aside. Grate the cheese.
3. Preheat the oven to 200°C/400°F/Gas Mark 6. Smear the base of an ovenproof baking dish of suitable size with some of the tomato sauce. Then cover with a layer of courgettes. Season lightly with salt and pepper, and sprinkle with some Parmesan. Repeat the process, starting with a layer of tomato sauce, seasoning lightly each time. Top it off with the last of the Parmesan.
4. Put the dish on the top shelf in the oven for about 20 minutes or until it displays an inviting crispy brown top.

Red Bean Chilli

Serves 2-3

Meredith tells me these are called *kidney beans* in America and she didn't like the ones on offer when she was growing up in Chicago. With any luck, things have changed!

Adapted from Rose Elliot's *The Bean Book*, this is a simple solution for people who don't eat meat but like the look of chilli – leave out the *carne*! After experimenting with variations – the addition of cumin powder and even Dijon mustard – I settled for *the simpler the better*. Quickly done, it tastes even better the next day. Don't forget the lemon!

1 onion – peeled and chopped
1 clove of garlic – chopped
2 tbsp olive oil
1 tsp chilli/cayenne powder
1 x 400 g/14 oz tin of tomatoes – chopped, with all the juice
450 g/1 lb red beans (from a jar or tin)
salt and pepper
juice of ½ lemon or more to taste

1. Soften the onion and garlic gently in the oil, stirring often.
2. Add the chilli (or cayenne) powder and the chopped-up tomatoes with their juice. Mix these all together, blending in the tomatoes.
3. Add the beans and season with salt and pepper. Bring gently to a simmer and cook, covered, for 15 minutes.
4. Pour over the lemon juice and mix in.
5. Serve over some basmati brown rice with perhaps a bowl of the Cumin Yogurt Sauce (page 62).

Helen's Spicy Cauliflower

Serves 3-4

Our friend Helen Richmond is an insouciant cook, a quality I have yet to achieve. She will throw some of this and a little more of that into her tall saucepan and very quickly the aroma of a delicious lunch fills her kitchen.

A neighbour's gift of a large cauliflower sat on her counter begging attention one morning we were there. Helen made a sauce of olive oil, paprika and lemon juice to bathe it in before roasting it in a moderate oven for 40-odd minutes. She served it with slice of pork fillet roasted with rosemary from her garden. The cauliflower dish turned out to be one of those you find your fingers sneaking back to when the hostess isn't looking. *Ju-ust* one more little piece... uum! Helen says that she's happy for me to reproduce the recipe here.

Don't expect much to be left over! Meredith, not usually a fan, gave it the thumbs up as the best cauliflower dish she'd tasted.

2 tbsp olive oil
1 tsp paprika – sweet smoked if you have any on hand
juice of ½ lemon – plus a little extra water (I noticed Helen
    fill the squeezed lemon halves with water and squeeze them
    out again, getting the most out of a lemon!)
1 cauliflower – stem removed and split into smallish florets
salt and pepper

1. Preheat the oven to 170°C/325°F/Gas Mark 3. In a large bowl, whisk the oil, paprika and lemon juice together into a dark red viscous sauce.
2. Add the cauliflower florets to the bowl and turn them over and over in the sauce. Sprinkle with salt and pepper.
3. Spread them out in a shallow roasting tray. Roast in the oven for about 40 minutes.

Cabbage and Red Lentils

Serves 4

After a night that registered -10°, a bowl of something gently spicy and soupy for lunch was just the ticket – a quick excursion to the East. Rose Elliot found this in Julie Sahni's *Classic Indian Vegetarian Cookery* and adapted it. I have tweaked it a bit. There was a small cabbage in the fridge and some fenugreek seeds on the shelf in the larder, which I whizzed into powder in a converted coffee grinder. (The fenugreek is optional but interesting. As its name implies, this herb is found in the Mediterranean region and has healing qualities as well as culinary uses.)

250 g/8 oz red lentils
1300 ml/2¼ pints stock
⅓ tsp turmeric
375 g/12 oz tinned tomatoes – chopped
1 tbsp olive oil
1½ tsp black mustard seeds
1 tbsp curry powder
¼ tsp fenugreek powder (optional)
1 onion – peeled and chopped
1 small cabbage – outer leaves removed, quartered, cored and
    shredded
salt and pepper
juice of ½ lemon
parsley, or even better still fresh coriander – chopped to
    sprinkle over

1. Rinse the lentils thoroughly. Put them in a saucepan with the stock and the turmeric and bring to the boil. Cook at a gentle simmer for 45 minutes.
2. Add the chopped tomatoes then set aside.
3. Heat the oil in a different pan. Add the mustard seeds and cook them until they start to pop – a couple of minutes.
4. Mix in the curry powder and the fenugreek (if using) and let them cook for a few seconds. Add the onion and the cabbage and mix everything together well. Cover the pan and cook for 5 minutes.
5. Add the wilted cabbage to the lentils. Bring the mixture up to a simmer, and leave to simmer gently for 20 minutes.
6. Season to taste with salt and pepper. Stir in the lemon juice. Sprinkle over the parsley or coriander. It's best served hot.

Fennel au Gratin

Serves 2 as a main course, 4 as an accompanying vegetable

I bought some impressive looking fennel at the organic market. It sat on the kitchen island demanding attention. I sliced one to eat raw at lunch after pasta, with a piece of Parmesan or pecorino and some of the new olive oil. It was tenderly crunchy, not in the least stringy.

Now what? Fennel au gratin, I thought – supper with a sweet potato and Tarator sauce (page 66). I'd never cooked it before and my search for guidance led me to the *Riverfood Farm Cookbook*. Rosemary and garlic was suggested with cream and Parmesan. I have substituted coconut cream and added more Parmesan. The difference between coconut milk/cream and cream of coconut? Coconut cream has the consistency of milk; it is *not* sweetened and it does not taste of coconut!

The dish can be prepared beforehand and set aside, covered with foil, then cooked an hour before you're ready to eat.

500 ml/1 pint stock to blanch the fennel
4 largish fennel bulbs – cleaned, cored and sliced vertically in
   1-cm/½-inch pieces
160 ml/5 fl oz coconut cream
3 cloves of garlic – peeled and crushed with a knife
1 tsp rosemary needles – chopped fine
salt and pepper
½ tbsp Parmesan cheese to mix in with the cream – more for
   topping, 1 tbsp perhaps

1. Bring the stock to the boil in a wide, shallow pan. Add the fennel slices and cook for about 5 minutes – until they begin to soften. Remove to a bowl with a draining spoon and let them cool a little.

2. Combine the coconut cream with the garlic and rosemary in a small pan and gently bring to the boil. Turn off the heat. Season this mix and add half the cheese. Pour it on the fennel and turn it all over thoroughly. Put the gratin mix in an ovenproof dish and cover with foil; it is now oven-ready.

3. An hour or so before you are planning to eat, heat the oven to 180°C/350°F/Gas Mark 4. Put the dish in the oven and cook for 30 minutes.

4. Take it out and lift off the foil. Sprinkle over Parmesan to cover and put it back, uncovered, in the oven for a further 15 minutes. It will brown nicely on top.

Cauliflower, Leek and Chickpea Curry

Serves 3-4

The other night I was looking for something easy to cook, preferably in a single pot; a ladleful of taste over some basmati brown rice – comfort food that cooks itself. I looked in the fridge and, as happens regularly, found a cauliflower (in good condition!) and a leek, and a bottle of chickpeas on the shelf in the larder. I knew there were a few small tomatoes left to gather at the end of the garden – perfect!

1 onion – peeled and chopped small
2 cloves of garlic – chopped
2 tbsp olive oil
1 tsp black mustard seeds
1 tsp each turmeric, cumin powder, ginger powder
½ tsp each coriander power, cayenne powder
250 g/8 oz tomatoes – chopped roughly
salt and pepper
500 ml/1 pint stock
1 leek – cleaned and sliced
1 cauliflower – separated into bite-size florets
3 tbsp cooked chickpeas – from a tin, can or bottle
2 tbsp whisked low/no-fat yogurt or coconut cream (see page 92)

1. Sweat the onion and garlic in the olive oil until they soften and begin to colour.
2. Add the mustard seeds and let them cook for a minute. Add the rest of the spices and mix them in.
3. Add the tomatoes, stirring them into the spice mix and season with salt and pepper. Cook for 5 minutes to break them down a little and form a sauce.
4. Add half the stock and cook for a further 5 minutes, reducing it a little.
5. Mix in the sliced leeks and the broken-up cauliflower – you may find you only need half the head – making sure the vegetables are immersed in the liquid.
6. Cook on a low heat for 30 minutes, checking now and then in case it's drying up, as it very nearly did for me! Add more stock as you need and cook on.
7. Add the chickpeas and cook for a further 5 minutes.
8. When the vegetables are tender, turn off the heat and let it cool down. Fold in the yogurt or coconut cream. Gently reheat to serve over some basmati brown rice.

Broccoli Parmigiano

Serves 2-3

An autumn/winter replacement for the Italian classic, *parmigiana melanzane*, and comfort food for the new chill.

450 g/1 lb broccoli – broken into florets
2 tbsp olive oil
salt and pepper
4 tbsp Quick Tomato Sauce (page 64)
Parmesan cheese – freshly grated

1. Steam the broccoli florets until they are beginning to soften but retain a good crunchiness.
2. Put them in a bowl and pour over the olive oil and season.
3. Heat the grill and char the florets lightly.
4. Preheat the oven to 200°C/400°F/Gas Mark 6. Oil a shallow ovenproof dish and spread some tomato sauce over the base. Cover with a layer of broccoli florets. Sprinkle over some Parmesan. Repeat the process finishing with a layer of Parmesan. Dribble some olive oil over the top. Pop the dish in the oven and bake for 15 minutes. It should come out sizzling.

Turkish Spinach and Rice (Pirincli Ispanak)

Serves 2+

A simple one-pot dish of spicy spinach with a modicum of rice for ballast, this is adapted from a recipe posted recently by Martha Rose Shulman in the *New York Times*. Traditionally it is served with Cumin Yogurt Sauce (page 62) which helps neutralise the sometimes tooth-tingling after-effect of the spinach.

450 g/1 lb fresh spinach – washed and drained of surplus water
2 tbsp brown basmati rice – washed and soaked in cold water
   for 30 minutes
2 tbsp olive oil
1 small onion – peeled and chopped
2 cloves of garlic – chopped
1 tsp sweet hot smoked paprika
½ tsp cinnamon
3 tinned tomatoes – about 100 g/4 oz – chopped
2 tbsp lemon juice – about a lemon's worth
3 tbsp water or stock

1. Steam the prepared spinach, covered, for a few minutes until it starts to wilt. Remove from the heat.
2. Drain the rice and cook it - salted and covered - in enough water to cover it by a thumbnail. It should take about 25 minutes. Set aside.
3. Heat the oil in a pan and gently soften the onion for a couple of minutes before adding the garlic. Cook for a further couple of minutes.
4. Add the spices and tomatoes and cook for a further 5 minutes, making a sauce.
5. Add the lemon juice, water or stock, spinach and rice, and mix together. Cover and cook on a low heat for 15 minutes.

Green Lentils with Spinach

Serves 4

A big glass jar of dry green/grey Puy-type lentils has sat on the shelf in the larder for months seeing no action. Inspired by a recipe in Rose Elliot's *Bean Book* that combines lentils and spinach (and remembering the pound-plus of beautiful organic spinach in the fridge), I gleefully took it down the other night.

This is another one-pot meal, though some brown basmati rice makes a good companion!

250 g/8 oz green/grey lentils – washed thoroughly but no
  need to soak them
water to cover the lentils by 2.5 cm/1 inch or a bit more
2 celery sticks – washed
1 large onion – peeled, ½ of it chopped
2 cloves of garlic – peeled, 1 pulped with ½ tsp salt
1 tbsp olive oil
1 tsp cumin powder
1 tsp coriander powder
450 g/1 lb spinach – washed and drained (use frozen if you
  like, thawed and squeezed)
couple of pinches of salt
juice of 1 lemon

1. Put the lentils in a pan with the water. Add the celery, whole onion and whole garlic. Bring to the boil, turn the heat to low and cook, covered, until the lentils are tender. Try not to overcook them to mush. The time depends on the age of the lentils – about 25 minutes – but keep an eye on them.

2. While the lentils are cooking, heat the oil in a sauté pan and add the chopped onion and garlic. Cook gently until they are soft and beginning to colour. Add the cumin and coriander and cook for a minute or two longer.

3. Remove the celery, onion and garlic from the lentils and drain the lentils of most of the excess liquid. Add the spiced onion and garlic mix and turn it all over to coat the lentils.

4. Meanwhile, put the spinach in a large saucepan with a couple of pinches of salt snuck in between the leaves – no extra water is needed. Cook on the lowest heat, covered, until it has wilted. Drain it of excess water but don't squeeze it.

5. Add the spinach to the lentils and squeeze over the lemon juice. Turn it over carefully and serve with some rice on the side and couple of lemon quarters on the plate.

7
Fish

People living on the Japanese islands of Okinawa eat fish at least three times a week. This is often cited alongside the fact that the islands boast an impressive number of centenarians – anecdotal evidence to support the solid clinical evidence that eating fish two to three times a week is beneficial to your health.

Fish is high in protein and low in saturated fat. Oily varieties like mackerel, sardines, herring, pilchards, trout and salmon are full of omega-3 oils that can help to lower heart rates and blood pressure and reduce the risk of heart attacks and strokes. These tasty varieties are often cheaper than their white-fleshed cousins.

But not everyone likes fish. 'Too many bones.' 'The heads put me off.' 'How do you cook it?' 'It's hard to find really fresh fish.'

The recipes here are not complicated and may help to persuade the unconverted.

'Fast Tracked' Fish Fillet calls for little preparation and is cooked in 5–10 minutes with a built-in sauce. Sautéed Mackerel with Rosemary and Garlic is another simple example. Go fish!

Fish in Crazy Water

Serves 2

Crazy title – simple and delicious recipe. Just fresh fish – whole (preferably) or in fillet form – poached briefly in water, flavoured with sweet cherry tomatoes, garlic, chilli and parsley. Fishermen on the Amalfi coast cook the unsaleable fish with these simple ingredients. Nothing 'crazy' about that!

Sometimes in winter cherry tomatoes on the vine can be surprisingly sweet. Later in the year any ripe tomato would do.

1 whole sea bream/dorade or sea bass, weighing about 450 g/
   1 lb – gutted and scaled
salt and pepper
4 tbsp olive oil
3 cloves of garlic – chopped
2–3 small dried red chillies – sliced roughly
450 ml/16 fl oz boiling water
250 g/8 oz cherry tomatoes
1 tbsp parsley – chopped

1. Wash the fish, pat dry and season.
2. Heat the oil in a pan large enough to hold the fish lying flat. Sauté the garlic and chilli together for a couple of minutes. Add the fish and sauté for half a minute each side.
3. Add the hot water, tomatoes and parsley. Squeeze the tomatoes against the sides of the pan to release their sweetness. Spoon some of the liquid over the fish, cover and cook on a low heat for about 10 minutes – depending on the size of the fish.
4. Carefully lift the fish out of the pan to a warm plate and separate the fillets if it's a whole fish.
5. Serve with two or three spoonfuls of the tomatoey sauce.

'Fast Tracked' Fish Fillet

Serves 4

This fabulously fuss-free fish fillet recipe I found in a Leon's (Restaurant, in London) cookbook. The fillet is cooked fast at the highest temperature the oven can reach. How can this work without the fillet shrivelling to a cinder? The answer's the lemon! It takes 10 minutes and the result is a delicious, succulent piece of fish with a modest 'built-in' sauce. Served on a bed of spinach, Swiss chard or a simple side salad of rocket, this is a useful dish for when you have company.

4 thick fish fillets
3 tbsp olive oil
a handful of parsley – chopped
salt and pepper
1 or 2 lemons – sliced thick (you need 2 or 3 slices per fillet,
   depending on the size of the lemons and the fillets)

1. Place an empty oven tray, large enough for the number of fillets you are cooking, on the top shelf. Heat the oven to the hottest temperature – yes, you're heating an empty tray! Meanwhile wash and dry the fillets.
2. Mix the oil and parsley together and turn the fillets in this mixture. Season them well.
3. Very carefully, as it'll be very hot, take the tray out of the oven and place the fillets on it. Place the lemon slices on top of the fillets.
4. Put the tray back on the top shelf of the oven for 10 minutes – less if the fillets are relatively thin.
5. When they are ready, serve them, suggesting that diners press gently down on the hot lemon pieces. Have more olive oil available on the side.

Monkfish with Black Olives in a Smoky Paprika Tomato Sauce

Serves 2-3

I'd wanted to cook this lightly spiced dish for ages; it is relatively simple to do. Marc Gayraud – my fishmonger in Castres market Tuesdays and Saturdays – was offering some medium-size monkfish the other morning at a reasonable price (18 euros a kilo). *Vendu, Monsieur! (Sold!).*

You can prepare the sauce beforehand and reheat it when you are ready to add the fish. That's the beauty of it. A little brown basmati rice and a seasonal green vegetable will make a pretty plate.

1 onion – chopped
3 tbsp olive oil
2 cloves of garlic – chopped
3 large tinned tomatoes or 250 g/8 oz fresh ripe tomatoes – chopped small
½ tsp cayenne pepper
½ tsp smoked paprika
sprigs of parsley and thyme
1 bay leaf
1 tsp salt
1 glass dry white wine
10 juicy black olives – stoned and halved
300 g/12 oz cleaned monkfish (ready to cook) or other firm fleshed white fish – cut crosswise through the cartilage in bite-size pieces

1. Soften the onion in the oil using a sauté pan large enough to hold the monkfish - about 5 minutes.
2. Add the garlic and cook for a further 3–4 minutes.
3. Add the tomatoes (which you have broken up) with the spices, herbs and salt. Cook these gently for a couple of minutes.
4. Add the wine and cook for another couple of minutes. This makes the simple base in which to cook the fish.
5. A few minutes before you want to eat, reheat the sauce and add the olives. Slide the monkfish pieces under the sauce and cook over low heat, covered, for 5–10 minutes until the fish is opaque and you can't wait any longer!
6. Serve over basmati brown rice with perhaps some steamed broccoli on the side.

Smoky Spanish Fish Stew

Serves 2

The smoky paprika and saffron flavours in this dish, adapted from the marvellous Moro stable, are subtle and light. They make it hard not to finish the lot in one go.

1 large sweet/mild onion – chopped
4 tbsp olive oil
2 cloves of garlic – chopped
1 tbsp fresh rosemary – very finely chopped
3 bay leaves
450 g/1 lb tomatoes – skinned and chopped – or 1 x 425 ml/14 oz tin of tomatoes – drained and chopped
½ tsp smoked paprika
salt and pepper
150 ml/6 fl oz white wine
a good pinch of saffron threads – soaked in 4 tbsp hot water
100 ml/4 fl oz stock – I use ½ an organic vegetable stock cube
100 g/4 oz blanched almonds – blitzed into powder or use powdered almonds – to thicken the sauce
450 g/1 lb pollock or other fish that holds its shape – fresh as can be and cut into chunks
250 g/8 oz mussels – cleaned
4 good prawns – unpeeled

1. Fry the onion in the oil until it's nicely coloured. It's worth the time involved, about 15 minutes, as this is the engine room of taste in the dish.
2. Add the garlic, rosemary and bay leaves and cook for a further 5 minutes.
3. Mix in the tomatoes and the paprika, season with salt and pepper and cook until the tomatoes have dissolved into a sauce – about 10 more minutes.
4. Add the wine and give it a minute or two before stirring in the saffron in water and the stock. Bring it all up to a gentle simmer then stir in the powdered almonds.
5. Fold in the fish, mussels and prawns. Cover the pan and cook for a further 5–10 minutes, turning everything over in the sauce from time to time.

Pollock with Rosemary, Lemon Slices and Tomato

Serves 2

A variation on a recipe from *The River Café Cook Book Easy*. I've substituted pollock for monkfish and added a sliced tomato, which melds well with the oil, anchovy and lemon base. Sweet little cherry tomatoes, halved, add colour and taste.

We had a fennel, radish and celery salad with these for lunch – dressed with a tablespoon of lemon juice blended with half a teaspoon of Dijon mustard, seasoned and then mixed with 3 tablespoons of olive oil.

1 lemon – sliced thinly
salt and pepper
3 tbsp olive oil
a good handful of rosemary sprigs
2 pollock steaks – rinsed and patted dry (you could try fillets, though the bone in the steaks adds flavour)
2 anchovy fillets – mashed to a pulp
1 largish tomato – sliced thinly (you can use a couple of tinned tomatoes – roughly chopped)

1. Heat the oven to 220°C/425°F/Gas Mark 7. Put the lemon slices in a bowl and season them with salt and pepper. Add a tablespoon of olive oil and mix carefully but thoroughly.

2. In a small, shallow oven tray, heat about a tablespoon of olive oil over a low flame. Spread the rosemary over the base. Place the fish steaks on top and season lightly. Spread half the anchovy pulp on each and cover them with the lemon slices. Arrange the tomato slices round the outside and drizzle the remaining tablespoon of olive oil over them.

3. Roast in the middle of the oven for about 10 minutes – the time depends on the thickness of the steaks.

No Potato Fishcakes

Serves 2 as a main course/4 as a starter

Always eagle-eyed for versions of fishcake made without potatoes (which I prefer to avoid), I spotted these a few years back in an article by Gordon Ramsay. I've added an egg to lighten them a little. We had them for lunch on a rainy day, with a simple green salad, and a dollop of tzatziki.

200 g/7 oz salmon fillet – skinned and checked for bones
200 g/7 oz smoked haddock – undyed if possible and skinned
handful of dill or parsley – chopped
2 small shallots – chopped very fine
salt and pepper
1 egg – lightly beaten
olive oil for sautéing

1. Cut both fish fillets into chunks and put them in a food processor. Pulse to a coarse mince – too much and it will be a slurry.
2. In a bowl, mix the fish with the dill or parsley, shallot, salt and pepper, and check the seasoning.
3. Fold the egg into the mix. Form into little patties or 'cakes'.
4. Chill them for an hour if possible – it helps them keep their shape.
5. Heat a tablespoon of oil in a large pan. When it's hot (important), slip a few of the 'cakes' into the pan and gently press them down a little. Sauté them on each side to a light brown finish – 2 or 3 minutes a side. They should still be moist inside.
6. Repeat the process until all the mix is transformed into these little wonders.

Sautéed Mackerel with Garlic and Rosemary

Another simple fish dish, this time with rosemary as the herb that informs. Mackerel, cooked whole in olive oil flavoured with the earthy tones of rosemary and garlic – good strong tasting elements to match the richness of the fish.

To be worthwhile, mackerel has to be fresh – nice clear eyes and firm to the touch.

2 medium-sized mackerel – gutted and cleaned
4 tbsp olive oil
4 cloves of garlic – peeled
2–3 sprigs of rosemary
salt and pepper
juice of ½ lemon

1. Rinse and dry the fish. Heat the oil in a large sauté pan and fry the garlic cloves until they begin to colour.
2. Add the fish with the rosemary and brown gently on both sides. Season with salt and pepper, and squeeze over the lemon juice.
3. Cover and cook for about 15 minutes – checking for doneness by carefully lifting the flap of the cleaned belly. If it looks pink, continue cooking for a couple of minutes more.
4. Take the mackerel out of the pan and lay them on the waiting plates. Spoon over the juices and watch out for the bones! Serve with extra lemon quarters.

Sea Bream with Garlic, Thyme and Lemon

Serves 2

This is adapted from a recipe by Marcella Hazan.

4 tbsp olive oil
couple of tbsp flour – I use chickpea flour
salt and pepper
1 sea bream – 600 g/1 lb 5 oz or 2 x 250 g/8 oz – washed
   and patted dry
handful of fresh thyme – very hardy and easy to grow in pots
3 cloves of garlic – crushed
juice of 1 lemon

1. Heat the oil to hot in a pan large enough to hold the fish flat. Season the flour with salt and pepper. Turn the fish in the flour, pat off the excess and stuff the cavity with half the fresh thyme.

2. Add the bream and garlic to the pan and sauté the fish for 2 minutes each side – taking care when turning it over in the hot oil.

3. Turn the heat down to low. Add the lemon juice and the rest of the thyme and season both sides of the fish with salt and pepper. Cover the pan and cook until the fish is done, turning it over after 5 minutes. About 10 minutes should do, depending on the size of the fish.

4. Now comes the tricky bit – lifting off the fillets. Not too tricky in fact – quite fun and no matter if it breaks up, it will taste the same. Carefully ease the top fillet away from the backbone, and place it on the plate! Peel the backbone away from the remaining fillet and slide a fish slice underneath.

Salmon Fillets Baked in Spinach

Serves 2

Simon Hopkinson uses butter and vermouth in this simple recipe from his book *The Good Cook*. I'm trying it with olive oil and white wine which fits in better with our way of eating. The single pot and the short cooking time make it a useful quick lunch. The timings can vary depending on the thickness of the salmon fillets.

2 tbsp olive oil
1 shallot – chopped fine
2 tbsp white wine
300 g/10 oz spinach – washed, de-spined and spun free of water
2 salmon fillets – skin left on
salt and pepper
grating of nutmeg

1. Heat a tablespoon of oil in a pan with a lid. Sauté the chopped shallot for a couple of minutes to soften it. Add the wine and leave it to bubble a moment or two.
2. Lay a third of the spinach in the pan and place the salmon fillets over it. Sprinkle over some salt and pepper and a grating of nutmeg. Cover the salmon with the rest of the spinach. Scatter the remaining tablespoon of oil over the spinach and cover the pan. Cook for 7 minutes over a low heat.
3. Turn the heat off and leave the pan covered for 10 minutes before serving.

8

Chicken

Our friend Irv Molotsky in Washington recently put me onto a wonderfully carefree way to roast a chicken, developed by America's Test Kitchen. Simple and hands-off – well, the chicken needs a hand getting into the oven but that's about it!

Brush a medium-size chicken with olive oil and season it well with sea salt and black pepper. Stuff a couple of garlic cloves, a sprig of rosemary and half a lemon in the cavity. Put a roasting tray in the oven. Heat the oven to 230°C/450°F/Gas Mark 8.

Take the tray out, wearing a strong pair of oven gloves, put the chicken in it and pop the tray back in the oven for 30 minutes.

Then, without opening the oven, turn off the heat and leave the chicken for a further 30 minutes.

Take the chicken out of the oven and the pan. While the bird takes a well-earned rest, covered with foil, for 20 minutes, make a little gravy. Lift all but a spoonful of fat out of the pan and ease the remaining good bits, including the squeezed garlic cloves, into a sauce along with half a wine glass of white wine or water. Gently heat this on the hob, stirring to amalgamate the gravy. Hey presto! – carefree roast chicken!

Spatchcock Chicken with Lemons and Bay

Serves 4

To spatchcock is to remove the back and breastbone of a chicken in order to open it up and flatten it out, as you might do a book. This allows the bird to cook more quickly and evenly. All you need is a pair of poultry shears or strong scissors and the nerve to try it! (Or ask your butcher to do it for you.) It's ideal for serving four people: the bird divides easily into quarters, thus dispensing with the need to carve. You could use guinea fowl quarters instead.

1 chicken
2 lemons – halved
6 bay leaves
salt and pepper
3 tbsp olive oil

1. Hold the chicken breast down and cut along each side of the backbone and lift it out. Gently press the wings apart. This will create a 'V' shape. To flatten the bird, snip through the little bone at the apex of the 'V' and press the sides down. Cut away any bits of fat and gristle still attached to the carcass.

2. Squeeze the juice from two lemon halves into a pan, halve them and leave the quartered lemon in the pan with the bay leaves.

3. Rub the skin of the chicken with the two remaining lemon halves. Lower the spatchcocked chicken over the lemon halves and the bay. Season well and spoon the oil over the chicken. Add the other two lemon halves to the pan. Cook, covered, on a low heat for 30 minutes. Preheat the oven to 200°C/400°F/Gas Mark 6.

4. Uncover, spoon over some of the juice and place the chicken in the upper part of the pre-heated oven. Cook for 40 minutes, checking and basting a couple of times.

Chicken and Leeks with Lemons

Serves 2

This is a handy lunch or supper dish – for two here; but for four with the simple addition of two extra pieces of chicken and another leek.

It's adapted from a recipe in Nigel Slater's impressive tome *Tender* – a tour de force of loving care. More than just a book of recipes, it's an enjoyable account of what can be done with a limited garden space in the heart of a city.

2 tbsp olive oil
2 leg and thigh chicken pieces
2–3 leeks – outer leaves removed, washed and sliced into
 5-cm/2-inch stubs
salt and pepper
1 wine glass white wine
juice and zest of 1 lemon
2 tbsp parsley – chopped
500 ml/1 pint stock

1. Heat the oil in a pan and slip in the chicken pieces. Gently colour them on both sides on a low to medium heat – 8–10 minutes in all. Remove them from the pan.
2. Turn the heat to low. Add the leek stubs to the pan and turn them over in the oil. Cover the pan and cook the leeks until they begin to soften – about 5 minutes.
3. Season the chicken pieces and return them to the pan. Add the wine, lemon zest and juice, a tablespoon of parsley and the stock. Bring the pan up to the boil, turn the heat down low and cover the pan. Cook at a simmer until the juices run clear when you pierce a piece of the chicken – about 20 minutes. Check the seasoning and sprinkle over the remaining parsley.

Pot Roast Guinea Fowl with Cider, Fennel and Apples

Serves 4

This is more Northern France than Mediterranean – the butter and cider point to Normandy rather than Provence for its provenance. It is a practical all-in-one-pot dish to go with some brown basmati rice or quinoa. Adapted from Jenny Baker's handy *Kitchen Suppers*, it's a flavoursome way to cook guinea fowl – a gamier tasting alternative to chicken.

2 large apples (Cox's, Fuji) – peeled, cored and quartered
1 fennel bulb – outer casing removed and cut into quarters or eighths if large
½ tsp cinnamon powder
25 g/1 oz butter
1 tbsp olive oil
150 ml/¼ pint dry cider
1 guinea fowl – cut into 6 pieces (2 wings, 2 legs, 2 breasts – larger pieces stay moist better)
salt and pepper
2 tbsp no-fat yogurt – whisked smooth (optional but gives the sauce a little more depth)

1. Fry the apple and fennel pieces, sprinkled with cinnamon, in half the butter and oil for 5–10 minutes. Set aside with the juices in a bowl.
2. Boil the cider in the pan to reduce it to roughly 3 tablespoons and pour it over the apples.
3. Brown the guinea fowl pieces on a medium heat in the remaining butter and oil, seasoning them as you turn them over.
4. Return the apples, fennel and sauce to the pan. Cover the casserole and cook on a low heat for 30 minutes. The juices should run clear when the thigh is pierced – if they are still pinkish, cook a little longer.
5. Remove the guinea fowl pieces, the apples and fennel from the casserole to a warmed plate. Let the juices cool a little. Whisk the yogurt into the sauce. Carefully pour the sauce into a heated jug. Serve with brown basmati rice or quinoa.

Coquelet and Oranges

Serves 2

I was later to the market than usual one Saturday; my favourite chicken stall had sold out of medium-sized birds. There remained very large ones to feed a family or these neat little numbers she called *coquelets*.

A coquelet is a small chicken, aka poussin, though I've read that an American poussin is larger.

The one I bought that Saturday morning weighed two pounds, perfect for the recipe I remembered in Diana Henry's *Crazy Water, Pickled Lemons*.

A simple marinade and a quick roast made this an agreeable and easy supper for the two of us – a treat, in fact, with the oranges and lemon/lime twist in the marinade.

For the marinade
juice of 2 oranges plus the rind of 1
juice of 1 lemon or lime plus the rind
2 tbsp balsamic vinegar
2 cloves of garlic – peeled and crushed
2 tbsp olive oil
2 tbsp dried oregano
a few thyme sprigs
salt and pepper

1 small coquelet or small chicken (if you can't find a small
    chicken, a larger one could be spatchcocked, see page 116,
    to cut the cooking time)
2 oranges – quartered and then each quarter halved
1 sweet potato – sliced in rounds (optional)

1. Mix the marinade ingredients in a small bowl.
2. Put in the chicken, breast side down, and let it rest in the mixture for 3 or 4 hours – overnight if you can.
3. Preheat the oven to 180°C/350°F/Gas Mark 4. Put the chicken in a roasting tin surrounded snugly by the orange pieces and sweet potato slices (if using). Pour a little of the marinade over the chicken.
4. Roast in the oven for an hour or more, depending on the size of the chicken, basting with the marinade two or three times.
5. Let the chicken rest a little, keeping it warm under a sheet of foil.
6. Halve the bird from front to back, along the breastbone and the backbone; it's best done with kitchen shears. Remove the orange and sweet potato slices (if using) to a warm dish. Deglaze the pan with a couple of tablespoons of water, scraping off the sticky bits to dissolve them in the liquid. Heat this gravy/sauce through gently, while stirring. Pour over the plated half-a-chicken and sweet potatoes.

Sprightly Spiced Roast Chicken

Serves 4

Our friend and neighbour Julie Ide put me onto this recipe, which originated from Josceline Dimbleby.

The anti-inflammatory and antioxidant qualities of spices turmeric and cumin in the marinade are an added plus.

For the marinade
juice of 1 large lemon
2 tbsp olive oil
2 cloves of garlic – peeled and crushed
1 tsp turmeric
2 tsp cumin powder

1 free-range/organic chicken, weighing about 1.4 kg/3 lb
1 glass of white wine to make the sauce/gravy

1. Mix the marinade ingredients in a small bowl.
2. Put the chicken in a large bowl and pour/brush/smooth the marinade over. Turn the bird in the marinade and leave for a few hours, covered, in the fridge.
3. Preheat the oven to 180°C/350°F/Gas Mark 4. Bring the chicken to room temperature. Sprinkle some salt over the bird and place it, breast down, in a large roasting pan. Pour any marinade remaining in the bowl over the chicken. Add a further tablespoon of olive oil. Place in the middle of the oven. Roast for 45 minutes, basting it from time to time with the juices.
4. Turn the bird over and roast for a further 30 minutes.
5. Let the chicken rest while you make a sauce from the juices. Tip the pan and spoon out all but a tablespoon of the fat. Add the white wine and stir, dissolving the 'bits' into the sauce over a low heat.

Braised Rabbit with White Beans, Garlic, White Wine and Parsley

Serves 4

Some people don't like the idea of eating rabbit – memories of treasured pets linger in the mind. However, rabbit is tasty, lean meat and makes for a change. You could also try this recipe with chicken.

4 tbsp olive oil
4 or more rabbit pieces
salt and pepper
½ tsp coriander seeds – dry roasted in a small frying pan and crushed
8 cloves of garlic – peeled
2 bay leaves
100 ml/3½ fl oz white wine
300 ml/10 fl oz water
1 large jar/tin white beans – cannellini, haricot or other white beans, drained
2 tbsp parsley – chopped

1. Preheat the oven to 150°C/300°F/Gas Mark 2.
2. Heat the olive oil in a lidded pan or casserole that can go into the oven. Season the rabbit pieces with salt and pepper and brown them gently.
3. Add the coriander seeds and garlic and turn them over in the oil until the garlic colours a little. Add the bay leaves, wine, water and beans.
4. Cover the pan and cook in the low oven (cooking it slowly helps to keep the rabbit moist) for about 30–40 minutes. Check the doneness of the rabbit – the juices should run clear. Sprinkle over the parsley before serving.

Chicken Paillard

Serves 2

Back in the days when I used to frequent Italian restaurants in London, chicken paillard with a side order of spaghetti in tomato sauce was a regular choice. It was a speciality of the chef at La Famiglia in Chelsea, owned by the legendary Alvaro Maccioni:

'A lot of Italian restaurants in London have lost touch with their roots. I say to my chefs that if you can cook like your mother then you are a good chef, but if you can cook like your grandmother then you are a great chef.'

Sunday night was his night off. He and his family always watched *Poldark*, he told me. I was lunching there one day with Ralph Bates, villainous George Warleggan in the series. Alvaro approached our table looking grim, offended even.

'Whatsa these? Thees is not a right – you are 'ere widge your enemee?'

A couple of weeks later, Angharad Rees (aka Demelza) and I were at the same table.

A beaming Alvaro came over... 'That's a bedder. You are widge your whyfe!'

2 chicken breasts – fat removed
For the marinade, whisk together
2 tbsp olive oil
2 tbsp lemon juice
zest of 1 lemon
salt and pepper

For a simple sauce, whisk together
1 tbsp lemon juice
3 tbsp olive oil
salt and pepper

1. On a chopping board, lay out a sheet of cling film/plastic wrap at least twice the width of the breast you are about to beat. (Putting a folded dishcloth or drying cloth under the board helps to keep it in place.) Carefully place a breast in the middle of the sheet. Lay a second sheet of the same size over the breast. Using a rolling pin, mallet or similarly heavy kitchen utensil, beat the breast to flatten and widen it, taking care not to damage it. Repeat the process with the second breast.

2. Peel back the cling film and place the first breast on a large plate. Pour over some of the marinade evenly. Place the second breast on top and pour over the rest of the marinade. Move the breasts around a bit to coat them in the mixture and leave for half an hour.

3. Heat the grill or a large frying pan on top of the stove. Season the breasts and place them on the heat. Two minutes on each side should do it, though it depends on the thinness you've achieved; the thinner the quicker.

4. Remove to a serving plate and pour over some of the sauce. Spaghetti would now seem an indulgence. A fresh green salad is a good accompaniment and/or some white beans with a swirl of olive oil.

Spicy Grilled Chicken Breast

Serves 4-6

This is adapted from the Indian actress and cookery writer Madhur Jaffrey's recipe, whose spicy green beans (page 73) would be a good accompaniment. I've cooked from her BBC series cookbook *Indian Cookery* for many years. It may be out of print but is worth seeking out.

In the introduction she recalls her mother telling her that Madhur's passion for food dates back to the hour of her birth, when her grandmother wrote the sacred syllable 'Om' ('I am') on her tongue with a finger dipped in honey. She was observed smacking her lips loudly. Something we do regularly after eating from one of her recipes!

An overnight marinade in this delicious blend of familiar spices and a quick turn on a griddle makes these strips of chicken breast a handy lunch option. (You could also cook these in a hot oven – 220°C/425°F/ Gas Mark 7 for 10–15 minutes, depending on their thickness.)

1 kg/2 lb free-range boneless chicken breast – skin removed, cut into 2-cm/1-inch strips

For the marinade
5 tbsp olive oil
4 tbsp red wine vinegar
1 medium onion – roughly chopped
1 head of garlic – peeled and roughly chopped
2.5-cm/1-inch nob of ginger – peeled and roughly chopped
2 tbsp fennel seeds
2 tbsp ground cumin
2 tsp ground coriander seeds
8 cardamom pods
8 whole cloves
1 tsp ground cinnamon
20 black peppercorns
½ tsp cayenne pepper
2 tsp salt

1. Put the chicken strips in a bowl.
2. Liquidise the marinade ingredients in a food processor.
3. Add the resulting mush to the bowl. Turn it all over, making sure the chicken is well covered by the marinade. Cover the bowl and leave it in the fridge overnight.
4. Heat a griddle to hot and cook the strips in batches. Depending on the thickness, allow them a couple of minutes a side. Cut into one to test for doneness; if it looks too pink, let it cook on a few seconds more.

Chicken Buried in Red Cabbage

Serves 4-6

Red cabbage is a member of the cruciferous family of vegetables (the four petals of their flowers are in the shape of a cross), as are broccoli, cauliflower, Brussels sprouts, kale and bok choy. These are super vegetables, with many health benefits claimed for them.

This recipe has the advantage of being an all-in-one dish. The chicken stays beautifully moist buried under its warm blanket of collapsed red cabbage.

1 chicken – cut up into 8 or more pieces
1 largish onion – peeled and thinly sliced
2 cloves of garlic – peeled and roughly chopped
6 tbsp olive oil
1 red cabbage (at least 450 g/1 lb) – quartered, the white stem
  removed and thinly sliced
salt and pepper
8 tbsp red wine

1. Choose a casserole or terracotta pot large enough to hold the chicken pieces in one layer.
2. Soften the onion and garlic in the oil until they begin to colour – about 10 minutes.
3. Add the cabbage and coat it well with the oily onion and garlic mix. Cook for 15 minutes, turning it over from time to time as it reduces in volume, taking care it doesn't burn. Season the cabbage well then bury the chicken pieces underneath. Pour over the red wine and cover the pot. Cook for 40–45 minutes, turning the contents over from time to time, taking care it doesn't burn.

Spatchcock Quail

Serves 2-3

There's a light gaminess about quail, making a change from chicken and guinea fowl.

There are many ways to cook quail. You can marinade them or stuff them with countless variations of flavours. I have to thank our friend and fabulous cook Charlotte Fraser for this way. (I do snip their heads off here, which used to give me pause. In London, I know they are sold headless.) One and a half each is usually enough, though it depends on their size. The Cucumber and Red Onion Salad (page 56) nicely cuts the richness of the quail.

4 quail – spatchcocked (see method in recipe for Spatchcock Chicken with Lemons and Bay, page 116)

For the marinade
2 shallots – finely chopped
2 small dry red chillies – left whole
2 large cloves of garlic – peeled and finely chopped
small bunch of coriander – finely chopped
juice of 1 large lemon
3 tbsp olive oil
1 heaped tsp chermoula (see page 63)

1. Mix the marinade ingredients together, and rub them all over the quail. Put them in a bowl, cover and leave in the fridge overnight.
2. Remove the quail from the marinade and season well each side. Preheat the oven to 200°C/400°F/Gas Mark 6.
3. Lightly oil a sheet of foil in a shallow oven tray and lay the quail on top. Cook them in the oven for 20 minutes. Slide them under the grill for 7–8 minutes to crisp up a bit.

Pan Roasted Chicken with Cherry Tomatoes

Serves 4

A bowl of our cherry tomatoes waiting their turn reminded me of this delicious Marcella Hazan recipe – a different summer way with chicken. Their sweetness is balanced by the touch of bitterness offered by the little black olives from Nice.

1 free-range chicken – cut up in 8–10 pieces
1 tbsp olive oil
2 tsp rosemary needles – chopped fine
5 cloves of garlic – peeled and left whole
salt and pepper
100 ml/4 fl oz white wine
1 small dry red chilli – left whole (optional)
20+ cherry tomatoes
handful of olives

1. Trim any excess fat, tidying up some of the loose skin from the chicken.
2. Heat the oil in a large sauté pan with a lid. Add the rosemary and garlic. Put in the chicken pieces, skin side down, and sauté them over a medium high heat. Nudge them with a spoon after 2–3 minutes; when they move easily without sticking to the pan, look to see if they've nicely browned. At that point, turn them over and repeat on the reverse side.
3. When you have a pan of golden chicken pieces, season them generously and add the wine and the chilli if using. Let it bubble a little, then cover the pan and cook the chicken for about 30 minutes on a low heat, turning the pieces from time to time to keep them moist. Add a tablespoon or two of water if needed. Add the tomatoes and olives and cover the pan again.
4. Cook until the skins of the tomatoes show signs of splitting, but keep an eye on the breast pieces: if cooked too long, they'll become dry.

9

Meat

Recent studies in Australia and the US come to the conclusion that there's nothing wrong with eating red meat. But they put a limit on the amount. The National Health and Medical Research Council of Australia recommends a weekly limit of 450 g/1 lb, as does the American Institute of Cancer Research. In other words, a couple of slices of the succulent pork tenderloin here or a serving of the lamb with green and black olives, a couple of times a week.

Food guru Michael Pollan, whose mantra is 'Eat food. Not too much. Mostly plants', agrees. He writes in his entertaining short book *Food Rules:* 'It is worth searching out meat from animals raised feeding in pastures. The food from these animals will contain much healthier types of fat as well as higher levels of vitamins and antioxidants. You will pay more but if you are buying and consuming less, the cost won't be much higher. The meat will taste better too!'

Monsieur Fraisse, our butcher in Lautrec, knows where each of his animals has been raised and what they've been fed on. A luxury I know and not so easy when shopping in supermarkets. It's worth asking, though, if there's a butcher's counter at your supermarket.

Processed meats, on the other hand, those charcuterie delicacies so popular here in France, get nothing but a bad press.

There are fewer recipes in this section than any of the others; a reflection of the fact that we are eating less red meat.

Roasted Pork Tenderloin

Serves 4

It's all in the name! This is the tenderest part of a pork loin. A pound and a half will feed four easily, maybe six, and as tenderloins are usually of similar dimensions, this allows you to double-up easily. A good dish for company, and delicious cold.

1 tenderloin of pork – most of the fat cut away

For the marinade
1 clove of garlic – peeled and pulped with 1 tsp salt
1 tsp Dijon mustard
spears of a branch of rosemary – chopped
leaves of several thyme branches
salt and pepper
3 tbsp olive oil

1. Whisk the marinade ingredients in a large bowl. Bathe the tenderloin in them. Put it in a plastic box or bag and leave in the fridge overnight. Let it come back to room temperature before taking it out of the bag/box.
2. Preheat the oven to 200°C/400°F/Gas Mark 6.
3. To seal the meat, heat 1 tablespoonful of olive oil in an ovenproof pan. When hot, seal the tenderloin, turning as it browns. Put the tray in the oven and cook for about 20 minutes. After 15 minutes check it for doneness by gently pressing down on the meat with a finger or thumb. It should be supple but not too supple. You can slice into the centre of the loin to check too. Ideally the meat will have a faintly pinkish tinge, though if the juices run pink, cook on for a couple of minutes. Try not to overcook as this will render the meat leathery. You can use a meat thermometer, of course. The US Department of Agriculture recently lowered the temperature considered safe for pork to 145°F (63°C).

Spicy Sausage with Fennel

Serves 2-3

Sausages are an occasional treat for us. The spiciness of the sausages combines well with the melting sweetness of the fennel and the sautéed garlic.

4 medium fennel bulbs
1 garlic bulb – cloves separated and peeled
60 ml/2 fl oz olive oil
salt
450 g/1 lb spicy sausages (or any good quality sausage) – cut
  into wine-cork-size chunks

1. Remove the outer casing of the fennel and cut the bulbs into eighths vertically. Put them in a pan large enough to take them in a single layer. Scatter the whole garlic cloves among them. Pour over the olive oil and add a pinch of salt.
2. Sauté gently, uncovered, for half an hour, turning the fennel as it colours. Add 60 ml/2 fl oz water, cover the pan and continue cooking for about another half an hour, adding more water as needed. The fennel should end up meltingly tender, the water making a light sauce.
3. While the fennel cooks its second half hour, sauté the sausages gently in a separate pan, turning them as they colour.
4. Add them to the fennel and cook it all together for 5 minutes. Adjust the seasoning and serve over Chickpea Mash (*Delicious Dishes for Diabetics*, page 169) or what you will.

Butterflied Pork Chop

Serves 2

I couldn't think of the French word for 'butterfly' at our local butcher's the other day. The word was as elusive as the insect. *Pamplemousse* kept fluttering around my mind, which means grapefruit! *Papillon* is the answer of course

When I tried to demonstrate with my hands, starting them in the praying position then opening out like a butterfly, M. Fraisse looked flummoxed.

The idea of slicing a pork chop almost in half horizontally was new to me too. I'd read about it recently in the Food Section of the *New York Times*.

After much elaborate miming, M. Fraise understood, and was game to have a go. He carefully cut round the bone, freeing up the meat. With his left hand holding the boneless fillet down, he sliced into the meat with a sharp knife, working it through to leave a quarter of an inch uncut. He folded back the two halves – still connected – to reveal the 'butterfly'.

The advantage, apart from making a single chop go further, is that it cooks quickly (3 minutes each side), retaining a juiciness that sometimes escapes when cooking pork longer. The herb topping (suggested by the *New York Times*) looks good and is tasty, but leave it off if you like.

1 thickly cut pork loin chop – butterflied
salt and pepper
1 tbsp olive oil

For the herb topping
3 tbsp parsley
2 tbsp mint
1 tbsp chives
4 cloves of garlic – peeled and sliced finely
salt and pepper
1 tbsp lemon juice
4 tbsp olive oil

1. Pile the herbs and garlic together and chop them finely. Season to taste. Add the lemon juice. Stir in the olive oil.
2. Season the chop well with salt and pepper.
3. Heat the tablespoon of oil in a sauté pan to hot and slip in the chop. Turn the heat down to medium and leave the chop to cook for 3 minutes. Turn it over and cook for a further 3 minutes; the cooking time depends on the thickness of the butterflied chop. The juices should not run pink.
4. If you are using the topping, spread some over the chop at this point. Let it rest on a serving plate, covered with foil, for 5 minutes before slicing and sharing it.

Pork Loin with Red Wine Vinegar and Bay Leaves

Serves 4

This is smelling mighty good at this moment – gently simmering on the stove. A dish I'd bet Marcella Hazan ate regularly, growing up in Senatico on Italy's northeast coast.

Marcella married an American and left home with him to live in New York City in her early thirties. She claims she had never done much cooking before this. The family meals were cooked by her mother, her grandmothers, aunts – the usual story of an extended Italian family. Living with a new husband in a foreign land concentrated her mind, she claims, and she taught herself to cook. She says she remembered the way dishes smelt back in Italy and used this sense to judge if she was doing it right.

No memory of Grandma's cooking for me, but from the smell that's wafting my way, things seem to be on course!

Marcella cooks Italian/Italian not American/Italian and her books are wonderfully detailed.

There are just three ingredients here apart from olive oil and salt. It's a long slow cook.

2 tbsp olive oil
750 g/1½ lb piece of pork loin – more or less as required, the
  cooking time will be the same
salt
3 bay leaves
1 tsp black peppercorns
8 tbsp red wine vinegar

1. Heat the oil in a solid pan with a lid. Sear the meat (brown it) all over then salt it. Add the bay leaves, peppercorns and vinegar and cover the pan tightly. It's important not to lose too much liquid.

2. Cook for an hour and a half or longer on the lowest possible heat. (I cooked this for 2 hours; it was good but next time I'll reduce the time a little and use a diffuser.)

3. Take the meat out of the pan and keep it warm, covered with foil. Carefully spoon off the fat, leaving the good residue behind. Add 3 tablespoons of water and scrape off the bits in the pan. Warm the gravy through.

Pork Chops Braised with Rosemary, Garlic and Thyme

Serves 2

We had these on a bitingly cold winter's day after the weather persuaded me to change direction from the fishmonger to the butcher! Spare rib chops are tastier and less prone to dry out than loin chops and they are the cheaper cut. That's what I settled for after waiting an age for Monsieur Fraisse, our butcher, to finish chatting to his previous customer – the cold was getting to me! I learned this simple way by watching the irascible but effective chef Gordon Ramsay demonstrating it – breathlessly.

2 tbsp olive oil
salt and pepper
4 cloves of garlic – squashed with the flat of a knife, peeled
   and halved
2 spare rib pork chops
sprigs of rosemary and thyme

1. Preheat the oven to 200°C/400°F/Gas Mark 6.
2. Dribble some olive oil and sprinkle some salt on a shallow oven tray and add a couple of garlic cloves. Place the chops on top. Sprinkle them with salt and pepper. Strip the rosemary needles from the stem over the chops. Do the same with the thyme (not so easily done). Roughly chop the remaining garlic cloves and scatter on top of the chops. Dribble more olive oil over the oven ready chops.
3. Put in the higher part of the oven for about 20 minutes. The cooking time depends on the thickness of the chops. It's best to cut into them to check: the juices should run clear. The rosemary needles take on a nice crunchiness and are worth eating with a mouthful of meat, as is the garlic.

10
Pasta

Sunday supper is invariably pasta and we are quite conservative about it. A sauce that hits the spot time after time is hard to forgo. We will sit in front of a bowl of some new pasta dish looking at it doubtfully, the mutually unspoken thought running through our heads: it's not the one that hits the spot!

One that hit the spot for years and still does is the tomato, garlic and anchovy spaghettini here. The taste deepens over 25 minutes as the anchovies and garlic meld into the tomatoes and olive oil.

Another, recently rediscovered, is spaghetti with a simple sauce of garlic, lemon zest, chilli and a crumbled stock cube. This requires scarcely any cooking time.

We find that wholewheat pasta welcomes strong sauces like amatriciana and arrabiata.

Hazelnut Pasta

Serves 2

This is like a pesto pasta. You can prepare the nut mix beforehand and reheat it very gently when you come to cook the pasta; stress-free cooking, in principle!

Hazelnuts roasted are particularly moreish. Mixed with olive oil, chilli and garlic, and served, as here, with nutty wholewheat pasta, they are irresistible!

3 tbsp olive oil
1 tsp hazelnut oil – if available
2 cloves of garlic – pulped
2 small dry chillies – chopped
75 g/3 oz roasted hazelnuts* – chopped (I use the small
     container in a food mixer and pulse the nuts to control the
     finished size – crunchy little bits, not powder)
2–3 tbsp parsley – chopped
salt
200 g/7 oz wholewheat penne or spaghettini
3–4 tbsp saved pasta water
50 g/2 oz Parmesan cheese – grated
pecorino cheese – if available, a couple of tbsp bearing in mind
     its saltiness

1. Heat the oils in a pan and add the garlic. Colour it gently, taking care not to burn it. Turn off the heat and remove the garlic from the pan to prevent it burning – a sieve with a metal net does this safely – and let it cool.

2. Add the chilli to the warm oil in the pan. Gently reheat the oil and chilli in the pan. Add the hazelnuts and the parsley and cook briefly over a low heat – about 3 minutes. Turn off the heat and mix in the sautéed garlic.

3. Bring a large saucepan of water to the boil with a dash of salt. Add the pasta and cook it to taste. When the pasta is done as you like it, drain, remembering to save 3 or 4 tablespoons of the water.

4. Return the pasta to the warm pan you cooked it in and add the nuts, parsley, garlic and cheese(s) and mix thoroughly. Add the saved pasta water to loosen the sauce a little. Add salt to taste. Serve immediately (it cools down quickly), with extra cheese and a swirl of olive oil if you like.

*To roast the hazelnuts

Heat the oven to 180°C/350°F/Gas Mark 4. Spread the hazelnuts over a shallow oven tray and put in the oven. Check them after 5 minutes – it depends on their size how long they take. Taste one to check for crunchy doneness; roast them a little longer if you feel they need it. Let the nuts cool before processing them.

Penne Amatriciana

Serves 4

This is traditionally made with bucatini – a thick spaghetti with a hole in the middle; *buco* means hole! (*Osso buco*: bone with a hole!)

I have sometimes confused this sauce from the eastern borders of Lazio and Abruzzo with another sauce beginning with A – arrabiata (see page 153). Both are robust tomato-based sauces, both are fired up with chilli, as much or as little as you like. Arrabiata, which means 'angry', is vegetarian, and the other, Amatriciana, has pancetta or bacon as an ingredient.

I use penne as I haven't found wholewheat bucatini yet. (We eat wholewheat pasta. Its lower place on the glycemic index makes it healthier, which matters for people with diabetes. Meredith and I prefer it now. That said, I limit myself to pasta once a week.)

2 tbsp olive oil
1 red onion – peeled and chopped small
50 g/2 oz pancetta or bacon – chopped small
2 cloves of garlic – chopped small
2 small dry red chillies – seeds removed and chopped
2 tsp rosemary needles – chopped small
2 tbsp red wine
2 x 400 g/14 oz can/tin tomatoes – chopped and drained but
  retaining 3 tbsp of its juice
salt and pepper
350 g/12 oz wholewheat penne

1. Heat the oil in a sauté pan large enough to contain the cooked pasta at the end. Gently brown the onion, bacon and garlic. Take time to get a nice sticky, slightly caramelised, result (but not burnt!). Stir in the chilli and rosemary and cook for a couple of minutes.
2. Add the wine and let it bubble for a moment to burn off the alcohol. Add the tomatoes and extra juice and mix everything together thoroughly. Cook this on a low heat for about 40 minutes to achieve an 'unctuous' sauce. Season with salt and pepper.
3. Bring a large saucepan of cold water to a boil, Add a teaspoon of salt. Add the pasta to the boiling water and cook to your taste.
4. Drain the pasta thoroughly and add to the sauce. Turn it well in and heat through.
5. Serve hot in warmed bowls with Parmesan cheese to grate – and red wine with a bit of attitude! Portion control is the only challenge!

Helen's Penne with Cannellini Beans, Garlic and Sage

Serves 2
(Serves 4: 2 x quantity of beans and liquid;
add 100 g/4 oz more pasta)

Every November for a few years now we have 'helped out' at our friends Keith and Helen Richmond's olive harvest in the Tuscan hills, southeast of Florence. 'Helping out' means we sort the leaves and branches from the olives lying on the net-covered ground, after the team of five men have shorn one of the thousand trees at the farm of its precious load. It takes them about ten eight-hour days, depending on the weather, to finish. Helen cooked this delicious pasta after the last olive was in the basket and the picking was done for another year. Two of the team stayed to eat it with us, Lucio and Ivan. Both still had their own trees to harvest. I like to think they'd had the dish before and knew it was irresistible.

4 tbsp olive oil
8 cloves of garlic – peeled but kept whole
handful of fresh sage
2 small red (hot) dry chillies – chopped
1 x 200 g/7 oz tin white beans – drained but their liquid retained
4–5 tbsp stock – I use ½ organic vegetable stock cube in a
  mug of hot water
salt
200 g/7 oz wholewheat penne

1. Heat the oil in a large saucepan. Add the garlic and let it colour a little. Add the sage and chillies and let them cook for a few moments. Add the beans and cook gently for about 15 minutes, while adding the bean liquid little by little to make a thick runny sauce. Cook the mix a little longer, adding the tablespoons of stock – a couple at a time – to keep it loose without losing the thick viscous quality of the sauce. Some of the beans will melt into the sauce; they can be encouraged with the back of a spoon. Season with salt and taste.

2. Cook the penne in plenty of salted water until just tender. Drain the pasta. Add the pasta to the sauce and let it meld in. Helen doesn't serve grated Parmesan with this pasta. I like it, but it's up to you, of course. I poured over a little of the new olive oil we had brought back with us – naturally!

Penne with Cauliflower, Garlic and Anchovy Sauce

Serves 4

Cauliflowers look so appealing. Their pure white faces peeking through the outer leafing, daring you *not* to buy them. They usually have to wait a while to get cooked, often because their green cousin, broccoli, is an easier option. Steamed then seasoned, with olive oil and a little lemon juice poured over, broccoli is quick to do and adds a fresh colour to the plate. Here though, the patient cauliflower takes centre stage with a piquant sauce.

1 cauliflower – released from its casing, washed and broken into large florets
salt
8 tbsp olive oil
2 cloves of garlic – peeled and finely chopped
6 anchovy fillets – mashed
1 or 2 small red chillies (depending on your taste) – chopped, discard the seeds
300 g/12 oz wholewheat penne or farfalle
3 tbsp toasted breadcrumbs
2 tbsp parsley – chopped

1. Cook the cauliflower florets in salted boiling water until they are tender. Remove from the pan and set it aside, saving the water to cook the pasta in later.
2. Heat the oil in a saucepan and add the chopped garlic. Sauté it until it changes colour, then take the pan off the heat and add the anchovy mash and the chillies. Stir this into the sauce.
3. Mix in the cooked cauliflower, breaking it up into small pieces and mashing some of it. Cook it in the sauce for a couple of minutes, and set aside. You are going to gently reheat the mixture just before the pasta is ready.
4. Bring the cauliflower water back to the boil and cook the penne or farfalle to your taste. Drain and add it to the sauce in the pan, turning it over carefully but thoroughly.
5. Sprinkle over the breadcrumbs and parsley and serve from a heated bowl.

Spaghettini with Tomato and Anchovy Sauce

Serves 4

This is from the matchless Marcella Hazan and is probably my favourite pasta dish of all time – comfort food *par excellence*! What makes it so delicious is the anchovies – controversial little fish, not to everyone's taste. Here they deepen the taste without dominating. The ones preserved in salt are best. They dissolve more readily than those preserved in oil, but it's a business preparing them.

Since I was diagnosed with type 2 diabetes, we have eaten wholewheat pasta and now we prefer it. How *al dente* it's cooked is a matter of taste.

2 medium cloves of garlic – chopped
6 tbsp olive oil
4 anchovy fillets – chopped fine and pounded into a paste in a mortar with a pestle if you have one
2 good tbsp parsley – chopped
1 x 400 g/14 oz tin of tomatoes – chopped with their juice
salt and pepper
400 g/14 oz wholewheat spaghettini

1. Lightly sauté the garlic in the oil in a small saucepan until it colours. Take the pan off the heat and add the anchovies and parsley, stirring well to dissolve them in the oil. Add the tomatoes, and season with salt and pepper. Cook at a steady simmer for about 25 minutes, stirring regularly.

2. When ready, the sauce will be thickish and have a little pool of oil on top.

3. Cook the spaghettini in plenty of well-salted boiling water. Test for your preferred doneness. Drain, put in a heated bowl and add the sauce. Mix well and serve.

Penne Arrabiata

Serves 4

Farmhouse cupboard fare: olive oil, garlic, tomatoes, chillies, pasta and Parmesan – that simple! A classic example of the Mediterranean way of eating, which is in the news, again. It has barely been out of the news. Stories of people living to very advanced ages on Greek islands crop up with annoying regularity on the health pages; annoying in the sense that you immediately want to go there and get a slice of the action!

4 tbsp olive oil
3 large cloves of garlic – pulped in a mortar or press
4 small dried red chilli – chopped with their seeds (less or
    more depending on your tolerance and taste, but this is
    called 'angry' [*arrabiata*] penne!)
1 x large 800 g/28 oz tin of tomatoes – chopped with its
    liquid
salt and pepper
300 g/12 oz wholewheat penne rigate (the ridged kind, which
    picks up the sauce better)

1. Gently heat the oil in a pan large enough to take the pasta too. Slip in the pulped garlic and let it colour lightly. Add the chilli and the chopped-up tomatoes. Cook until the sauce thickens – about 30 minutes – stirring regularly. It should be a thick pool of red glory. Taste for heat/spiciness; add more if you like.
2. Bring a large saucepan of water to the boil and add a teaspoon of salt. Add the penne, stir to stop the pasta sticking to the base of the pan and bring back to the boil. Cook until it is just tender.
3. Drain well and add the penne to the sauce and turn to coat the pasta thoroughly. Serve with grated Parmesan if that suits, and a glass of hearty red wine.

Spaghetti with Garlic, Lemon Zest and Chilli

Serves 2

This is the quickest, delicious sauce, and so simple – made in 5 minutes while the pasta is cooking. Our friend Hilton McRae made it for us in London. My version is a slight twist on his, using olive oil instead of butter and adding lemon zest.

100 g/4 oz wholewheat spaghetti
4 tbsp olive oil
3 sprigs of fresh rosemary
3 cloves of garlic – pulped in a mortar or press
1 vegetable stock cube – crumbled
2 tbsp Parmesan – grated
zest of 1 lemon
some chopped parsley

1. Cook the spaghetti in salted water until al dente or to your taste.
2. Meanwhile, heat the oil in a small saucepan and on a low heat cook the rosemary sprigs and garlic until the garlic begins to colour – about 5 minutes.
3. Add the crumbled stock cube, stir thoroughly and turn off the heat.
4. Drain the pasta and put it in a warm bowl. Strain the oil through a sieve and add it to the pasta with the cheese. Turn it all over to coat the pasta with the oil and sprinkle the lemon zest and parsley on top. You could pick the not-too-brown garlic bits out of the sieve and scatter them over the pasta too!

11
Grains and Pulses

New takes on these ancient ingredients crowd newspaper food sections; restaurant chefs and café owners compete with scrumptious-looking grain and pulse 'salad' displays. Always an important feature of the Mediterranean way of eating, they offer healthy, affordable and tasty alternatives to the western 'meat and two veg' daily norm.

Grains and pulses like those in this book – white cannellini beans; red beans; chickpeas; red and grey-green lentils; red or white quinoa; pearl barley; basmati brown rice – all have their own particular textures and tastes, which distinguish them and complement the glamorous additions they are attracting nowadays.

Pearl Barley 'Risotto' with Leeks and Mushrooms

Serves 2-3

Traditionally risotto is made with Italian Arborio rice – a round variety that plumps up well as it absorbs liquid, while still retaining a bite at its centre. As white rice – a carbohydrate converting more quickly to sugar – it's not ideal for those with diabetes. Pearl barley is an acceptable substitute. It has a delicious nuttiness all its own while modestly hosting, in this case, the mushrooms and leeks.

This takes a little time but when you come to cook it, the zen of making risotto(!) kicks in and it becomes a quiet meditation followed by a satisfying chew. Risotto has the virtue of being a meal-in-one dish. This is adapted from an original recipe by Emma Booth who won a prize with it in *Stylist* magazine.

Dried mushrooms aren't always easy to find but they serve as a taste engine, adding depth to the dish. If you can't get dried mushrooms, just use 200 ml/7 fl oz warm water!

25 g/1 oz dried mushrooms
2 garlic heads – cloves separated but skin left on
4 tbsp olive oil
200 g/7 oz fresh mushrooms – sliced thin
1½ leeks – chopped fine
2 tbsp white wine
200 g/7 oz pearl barley – rinsed thoroughly until the water
   runs clear
1 tsp fresh thyme – chopped
500 ml/1 pint stock
50 g/2 oz Parmesan cheese – grated
black pepper and salt

1. Put the dried mushrooms in a bowl and pour over 200 ml/ 7 fl oz hot water. Leave to soften for 20 minutes. Strain into a bowl, reserving the liquid. Chop the softened mushrooms ready for use.

2. Heat the oven to 190°C/380°F/Gas Mark 5. Put the garlic cloves in a bowl and mix with a tablespoon of olive oil. Empty them onto a shallow oven tray. Bake for about 15–20 minutes until they are soft. Set aside to cool.

3. Peel the garlic and fork them into a mush. This is a messy business but it ends with a satisfying licking of the fingers.

4. Heat 2 tablespoons of oil in a pan and sauté the fresh mushrooms until they start to colour (this happens after they have released their moisture), then set aside.

5. Heat the last tablespoon of oil in a medium casserole (the one in which you will serve the risotto) and sauté the leeks over a medium heat until they soften and colour a little. Add the wine and let it evaporate, stirring the while. Mix in the pearl barley, thyme and cooked garlic mush.

6. Have the stock in a pan close by, simmering on a low heat. Add the stock a ladle at a time, stirring often, taking care the mix doesn't catch the bottom of the pan and burn, followed by the mushroom water (if you are using dried mushrooms) or warm water (if not).

7. When the barley is soft but still has a little bite in the centre (this took about 20 minutes for me), the risotto is ready for the dry and fresh mushrooms. Add them and stir in, followed by the Parmesan cheese. Season with black pepper and salt. Meredith recommended a sprinkling of parsley at the finish.

Warm Lentil Salad

Serves 4

This satisfying and comforting dish is adapted from Martha Rose Shulman's idea, spotted recently in the *New York Times*. She calls it a salad I guess because it is dressed with a vinaigrette – an interesting one. I topped the dish off with some plain soft goat's cheese. She suggested serving the lentils with roasted winter squash, so I chose pumpkin with spicy seasoning (see page 80). I like the addition of turmeric to the cooking lentils. It lends them a touch of mystery!

225 g/8 oz green lentils
1 tsp fresh ginger – chopped very fine
1 tsp turmeric
1 clove of garlic – peeled
1 small onion – halved
500 ml/1 pint water

For the vinaigrette
1 tbsp red wine vinegar
1 tsp balsamic vinegar
1 tsp Dijon mustard
1 tsp cumin powder
3 tbsp olive oil
1 tbsp walnut oil
salt and pepper

parsley – chopped

1. Combine the first six ingredients and bring to the boil in a pan. Simmer gently, covered, until the lentils are tender but not mushy. Drain off any excess water and empty the lentils into a bowl.
2. Mix the vinaigrette ingredients together in a bowl in the order listed, leaving aside the parsley. Turn this mixture into the warm lentils, taking care not to mush the lentils too much. Sprinkle the parsley over to finish.

Softening Dried Beans

Serves 1

I like a plate of beans, with olive oil swirled over them. There are good quality beans available now in glass jars which can be quickly heated up. But perhaps you have a packet of dry white beans that has spent some time on a shelf, daring you to do something with them. Ever present, silently reproachful, waiting for some action, they can be intimidating! The sooner they are treated, the better, and this way is simplest.

225 g/8 oz dry beans
1 tsp salt
½ vegetable stock cube
salt and pepper

1. Put the beans in a bowl and cover them with cold water. Leave to soak overnight.
2. Heat the oven to 170°C/325°F/Gas Mark 3. Drain the beans and rinse them. Put them in a medium casserole/pot/pan and cover them again with a top-of-the-thumb-joint of cold water. Cover the casserole and bring it to the boil. Place it on the middle shelf of the oven and leave for 40 minutes.
3. Test for softness, leaving it longer if necessary; the older the beans, the longer it will take. You can always add more hot water, not too much though as the liquid formed in the process can be used at another time. Add a teaspoon of salt to the casserole and leave to cool in the liquid.
4. When you are ready to eat, reheat them in a little of the liquid, adding half an organic vegetable stock cube, crumbled. Drain the beans and serve them hot. Season to taste with salt and pepper, adding a swirl of the best olive oil you have.

Chickpea, Leek and Fennel Curry

Serves 4

Rose Elliot's vegetarian cookbooks, *Not Just a Load of Lentils* and *The Bean Book*, have been on my bookshelves for ages and much thumbed! The recipes often chime perfectly with the way of eating encouraged in this book. This is adapted from one in *The Bean Book*. I made it in the morning and gently reheated it in the evening, giving the spices time to settle and meld. I served it with Lemony Lentils (page 170).

1 tbsp olive oil
1 tsp whole cumin seeds
1 small onion – peeled and chopped
1 clove of garlic – peeled and chopped
½ tsp powdered cumin
½ tsp powdered coriander
½ tsp each garam masala, turmeric, ground ginger
¼ tsp cayenne/chilli powder
1 tsp fresh root ginger – peeled and chopped (optional)
1 large jar cooked chickpeas – drained (the precise quantity isn't critical!)
1 large leek – damaged outer parts removed, cut down to the base, washed and sliced
2 fennel bulbs – outer leaves removed, the bulb quartered, then halved for a second time
500 ml/1 pint vegetable stock
2 tbsp parsley or coriander – chopped

1. Heat the olive oil in a pan. Gently fry the cumin seeds until they start to pop. Add the onion and garlic, and soften – about 3 minutes.

2. Add the spices and mix them in. Add the chickpeas. Add the leeks and fennel and mix.

3. Add the stock: start with half the quantity, then adjust as needed. Bring the mixture to the boil, cover the pan and simmer until the fennel is tender – about 25 minutes. Fold in a tablespoon of parsley or coriander. Sprinkle the second tablespoon of parsley or coriander over the dish when you serve it hot with Brown Basmati Rice (page 167) and a Cumin Yogurt Sauce (page 62).

White Beans with Tomatoes

Serves 4

This offers an advance on my favourite plate of comfort food. A simple plate of white beans with a swirl of the finest olive oil. It is what I would order in Mario's tiny restaurant across the square from the main market in Florence along with a veal chop, grilled to perfection. "Comfort food" is easy and quick to do, and passes the taste test.

A portion of steaming broccoli is often my choice to go with them.

2 tbsp olive oil
2 cloves of garlic – peeled but kept whole
a sprig of sage
3 ripe tomatoes or 3 tinned tomatoes – chopped with a little of their juice
250 g/8 oz dry beans – prepared as per p161 or a tin or jar of white beans, drained
½ vegetable stock cube – crumbled into a tbsp warm water
salt and pepper

1. Heat the olive oil in a pan and add the garlic cloves. Let them colour gently, flavouring the oil. Lift them out and add the sprig of sage to the oil.
2. Add the tomatoes and their juice and stir them in, to make a quick sauce.
3. Add the beans and the stock. Season with salt and pepper and cook, covered, on a low heat for 15 minutes. It will have transformed into lightly bubbling bean stew that demands tasting!

Garam Masala

Garam masala may be an ingredient new to some. *Garam* means hot and *masala* means a spice mix. The 'hot' is not a spicy hot but rather a heat that warms the body (in principle). I've learnt about this subtle and delicate mix from Kris Dhillon's *Curry Secret*. She writes: '... the theory comes from the Hindu concept of medicine and diet called *tridosha*, which teaches that some foods have a warming effect on the body while others have a cooling effect. Spices such as cardamoms, cloves, cinnamon and nutmeg are *garam* constituents of this aromatic mixture.'

Garam masala is usually added towards the end of the cooking process. It can also be sprinkled over cooked food to enhance the flavour. It is a mixture of spices that has infinite variations. You can buy it (just as you can buy curry powder) or you can easily and quickly make your own. This version is from the wonderful Indian actress and food writer Madhur Jaffrey, author of *Indian Cookery*.

1 tbsp cardamom seeds
5-cm/2-inch cinnamon stick
1 tsp cumin seeds
1 tsp whole cloves
1 tsp black peppercorns
½ small nutmeg – grated

1. Whizz all the ingredients to a fine powder in a spice or coffee grinder.

Sam's Quinoa

Serves 4

Quinoa is one of the oldest known grains and a useful alternative to rice. It takes less time to cook and is very easily digestible.

Sam Talbot is an American chef in his thirties, working now in Montauk, Long Island. He has type 1 diabetes and has written a delightful cookbook, illustrating the way he lives, eats and cooks, with a nicely ironic title, *The Sweet Life*. In his book he raves about quinoa; he eats it at least three times a week. This is his delicious recipe, slightly adapted. The amount of liquid required is double the volume of the quinoa – easy to remember! Leaving the coriander and cumin seeds whole gives a nice added crunchiness.

2 tbsp olive oil
1 shallot – chopped small
1 tbsp coriander seeds
1 tsp cumin seeds
2 tbsp fresh ginger – chopped small
4 cloves of garlic – pulped with some salt
170 g/6 oz red or white quinoa
470 ml/16 fl oz stock
zest and juice of 1 lemon
parsley – chopped

1. Heat the olive oil in a pan and sauté the shallot and the spices for about 5 minutes to soften them.
2. Add the quinoa to the pan and turn it over with the spice mix. Add the stock, lemon juice and zest and bring it to a simmer. Cover the pan and turn the heat down to low. Cook for about 20 minutes.
3. Check to see how it's doing after 15 minutes and give it a stir. The grain should absorb all the liquid by the end of cooking. Sprinkle the parsley over and fork it carefully into the quinoa.

Basmati Brown Rice

Serves 4

Brown basmati is my rice of choice. It is unrefined and tastes nuttily delicious. Everyone has their own way to cook rice. This is my method of the moment, introduced to me by our friend Simone Sarti.

250 g/8 oz basmati brown rice
½ tsp salt
bay leaf – if you have one to hand

1. Using a sieve, rinse the rice thoroughly. Rest the sieve holding the rice on the rim of a bowl full of water. Soak the rice in the water for 20 minutes or longer.

2. Life the sieve out of the water and empty the rice into a saucepan. Top the rice by roughly an inch of water. Bring up to the boil, add the salt and bay leaf and cover. Cook over the lowest heat possible – using a heat diffuser if you have one – for about 25 minutes, resisting the temptation to peek under the lid.

3. Check for doneness. Cook a little longer if necessary, then let it rest covered for 10 minutes.

Tari's Worry-Free Cumin Rice

Serves 4

In *Delicious Dishes for Diabetes*, I mentioned our friend Tari Mandair, 'the Carefree Cook', as an example to all us 'worryguts'. He is a Sikh and in that tradition's spirit of being of service to others often visits the Sikh Temple in Southall in west London to spend hours washing the dishes in the canteen there, which is open to all. Here is the simple cumin-flavoured rice I watched him cook for us recently.

1 tbsp olive oil
1 tsp cumin seeds
a mug brown basmati rice plus 2.5 x the volume of water
salt and pepper

1. Heat the oil and gently sauté the cumin seeds until they colour.
2. Add the rice and coat it in the oil. Season well with salt and pepper.
3. Add the water. Bring up to the boil. Turn the heat down to the lowest possible – use a heat diffuser if you have one. Cook for 40 minutes. Then let it stand, covered, for 40 minutes.

Spicy Chickpeas

Serves 4

These spicy little numbers made up a quick lunch recently, with grilled strips of marinaded chicken breasts and Swiss chard leaves sautéed with garlic and olive oil. This is adapted from a lovely book of recipes by Australian cookery writer Jody Vassallo.

2 tbsp olive oil
1 clove of garlic – peeled and crushed to a paste with a little salt
1 tsp each smoked paprika, cumin powder, white pepper powder, coriander powder, cayenne powder, dried thyme, dried oregano and salt
1 x 450 g/16 oz tin/bottle cooked chickpeas – drained, rinsed and dried (it's important to dry them well; kitchen paper comes in handy here)

1. Put a tablespoon of the oil, the garlic, spices and dried herbs in a bowl and add the salt. Mix these thoroughly with a fork.
2. Add the chickpeas and turn them over to coat them in the spice mixture.
3. Heat the remaining tablespoon of olive oil in a large frying pan. When the oil is hot, add the chickpeas and roll them about in the oil – they should ideally lie in one layer. Cook them over a gentle heat for 10 minutes, until they colour and crisp up.
4. The chickpeas are delicious served with a chicken breast each (cut into thin strips, seasoned and marinaded in olive oil for an hour), then cooked on a hot grill for a couple of minutes each side.

Lemony Lentils

Serves 4

Meredith tells me the first time she became aware of lentils was at the age of thirty-five. They had not been part of her experience growing up in suburban Chicago! Much has changed, Indian restaurants are commonplace now in the US.

This recipe is hands-on for the first half hour or so, as it builds in the taste. Then it chugs along on a low heat for 50 minutes as the lentils dissolve and the dal forms. The finish involves sautéing a small amount of onion, garlic and dried red pepper to stir into the mix to lift it. We ate it recently as an accompaniment to the Spicy Grilled Chicken Breast (page 126). It is adapted from a recipe in Ismail Merchant's excellent and quirky cookbook *Indian Cuisine*.

1 small onion – peeled and chopped
2 tbsp olive oil
225 g/8 oz red lentils – rinsed until the water runs clear
a short stick of cinnamon
1 tsp fresh ginger – grated
250 ml/½ pint (approx) stock
250 ml/½ pint (approx) hot water
1 tsp cayenne pepper
1 tsp salt
juice and the shells of a lemon

To finish
2 tbsp olive oil
½ small onion – sliced
1 small dried red chilli – chopped
1 garlic clove – peeled and chopped

1. Cook the onion over a low heat in the oil until it is opaque – about 5 minutes.
2. Add the lentils, cinnamon and ginger, and mix in. Cook these together gently for about 10 minutes, keeping the heat low and stirring from time to time to avoid them sticking to the bottom of the pan and burning. A nutty aroma starts to rise from the darkening lentils, as they cook.
3. Add the stock and hot water, cayenne and salt. Bring to a simmer. Cook gently for a further 10 minutes, then add the lemon juice and the empty lemon halves and stir it all together. Cover the pan and continue cooking on a very low heat – use a heat diffuser if available – for 45 minutes, stirring occasionally to avoid sticking.
4. In a small frying pan, heat the olive oil and add the sliced onion. Let this colour for 5 minutes over a medium heat. Add the chilli and chopped garlic and continue cooking until the garlic begins to brown. Add this to the lentils and mix it in.

12

Desserts

I don't eat desserts. Well, that's not the whole truth. Meredith sometimes makes a dessert for company that is so good that not to try it would be churlish.

I've never had a craving for large portions of exotic 'afters', though I remember the wonderful 'knickerbocker glories' (ice cream sundaes in the US) at Marshall and Snelgroves' lunch counter in the early 1950s – one of my grandmother's regular treats!

For others, with a sweet tooth, it's a sacrifice to forgo the third course and it's true that a good meal needs a grace note at the end to round it off; a contrast to the savoury tastes of the main dish and something that complements the coffee or tea to come.

For me, surprisingly, it's a piece of chocolate – with a high proportion of cacao (90 per cent!), now regarded as a healthy choice. One square, with a small cup of black coffee, is the perfect end to lunch; that, and a dried fig and a couple of dried apricots.

I've been on the look-out for simple seasonal ways to finish a meal for those with a yen for more than the above and less than the full catastrophe! Here are some of the ideas I found.

Peaches in Honey and Lime

Serves 4

A beautifully simple recipe by Frances Bissel, whose approach to cooking I find inspiring. The title of her book *The Pleasures of Cookery* says it all and could serve as a subtitle to this one. She loves to cook and is constantly finding original ways to treat seasonal ingredients.

2 tbsp water
1 tbsp runny honey
1 fresh lime – grated zest and juice
4 peaches – peeled and cut up

1. Heat the water and honey. Add the lime juice and zest. Gently bring to the boil. Turn off the heat and cool. Leave overnight. Pour the liquid over the peaches and leave in the fridge for a couple of hours.

Pear in Honey and Lemon

Serves 4

Another one from Frances Bissel.

4 pears – peeled with stalks left on
1 lemon – cut in half
4 dessertspoons runny honey

1. Rub the pears with the cut side of the lemon halves. Gently heat the lemon juice and honey in a small pan. When the honey has melted, add the pears. Cover the pan and cook gently for about 10 minutes to soften the pears. Leave them to cool. Serve with a little of the lemony syrup spooned over each pear.

Moroccan Orange Salad

Serves 4

This classic Moroccan dessert serves well after a rich main course. If you can find blood oranges, they make a good show.

4 oranges – peeled, pithed and sliced thin
2 tbsp orange blossom water
a few mint leaves – chopped
4 dates – stoned and chopped roughly
a sprinkling of cinnamon

1. Arrange the orange slices in a glass or white bowl. Sprinkle over the orange blossom water. Scatter over the mint and dates, and a shake of cinnamon. Refrigerate until the start of the meal.

Baked Apples

Serves 4

These showed up regularly at home in the 1950s. Large green cooking apples were always sitting around. I remember liking the puffiness of the apple flesh as it came out of the oven, scraping it away from the skin and mixing it with the syrupy sauce; my mother used golden syrup instead of honey.

4 large apples
a handful of raisins
rind of 1 lemon – chopped
a handful of walnut kernels – chopped
4 tbsp runny honey
4 cloves
100 ml/4 fl oz water

1. Heat the oven to 180°C/350°F/Gas Mark 4.
2. Core the apples but leave them whole. Arrange them on an oven tray.
3. Put some raisins, a pinch of lemon rind, a few walnut pieces, a tablespoon of honey and a clove in each cavity. Pour the water into the tray. Bake for an hour. Leave to cool.

Fresh Strawberries with Lime Zest and Mint

Serves 4

Our friend Romaine Hart brought this idea back from Los Angeles and passed it on. The three distinct flavours live happily together.

450 g/1 lb strawberries – halved
2 limes – zest lifted and squeezed
a handful of mint leaves – chopped small

1. Arrange the strawberries in a glass (for preference) bowl. Sprinkle over the juice and the zest of the lime. Scatter over the chopped mint leaves.

Baked Peaches

Serves 4

6 dried figs – chopped small
170 g/6 oz ground almonds
a little egg white
4 large peaches – stones removed and halved
50 g/2 oz flaked almonds

1. Heat the oven to 200°C/400°F/Gas Mark 6.
2. Mix the figs, ground almonds and the egg white. Using a teaspoon, fill the peach cups with some of the mixture. Sprinkle over some flaked almonds. Bake for 20 minutes.

Prunes in Red Wine

Serves 4

This is from our friend Conner Middlemann-Whitney's excellent anti-cancer cookbook *Zest for Life*. She's a 15-year cancer survivor and offers online Mediterranean diet and cancer prevention advice. She's also mad about prunes!

450 g/1 lb prunes – preferably from Agen and pitted
1 tbsp freshly grated ginger
zest of an orange
200 ml/7 fl oz freshly squeezed orange juice
100 ml/3½ fl oz red wine
1 cinnamon stick

1. Put all the ingredients in a small saucepan. Bring it gently to the boil and let it simmer for 15 minutes.
2. Turn off the heat and let it cool. Store in the fridge until 30 minutes before using.
3. Serve with some of its natural syrup and a dollop of yogurt.

Lina's Dried Fruit Compote

Serves 10

1200 ml/just over 2 pints water
2 rosehip teabags
400 g/14 oz prunes
250 g/8 oz dried apricots
350 g/12 oz dried figs
50 g/2 oz raisins
25 g/1 oz dried cranberries (optional if difficult to find)
5 cloves
1 cinnamon stick
50 g/2 oz flaked almonds
yogurt or crème fraîche

1. Boil the water, pour over the teabags in a china bowl and leave for at least 10 minutes to steep.
2. Discard the teabags and pour the liquid into a pan. Add the dried fruit and spices, and simmer for 15 minutes – until enough water is boiled off to leave a syrup on the fruit.
3. Leave to cool. Serve with the flaked almonds or toasted pine nuts and yogurt or crème fraîche.

My Favourite Dessert

Serves 1

1 perfectly ripe pear
a serving of pecorino cheese

1. Halve the pear from top to bottom. Pull away the stem. Halve each half again. Eat pieces of each at a leisurely pace.

The GI and the GL

The Glycemic Index (GI) is a measure, on the scale of 1 to 100, ranking carbohydrates according to their effect on our blood glucose levels and thus their post-meal impact.

The Glycemic Load (GL) is a measure of the impact of the glucose in a single *portion* of food.

The GI Foundation neatly sums it up thus:

'Not all carbohydrate foods are created equal, in fact they behave quite differently in our bodies. The glycemic index or GI describes this difference by ranking carbohydrates according to their effect on our blood glucose levels. Choosing low GI carbs – the ones that produce only small fluctuations in our blood glucose and insulin levels – is the secret to long-term health, reducing your risk of heart disease and diabetes and is the key to sustainable weight loss.'

Liquid Conversions

Imperial	Metric	American
½ fl oz	15 ml	1 tablespoon
1 fl oz	30 ml	⅛ cup
2 fl oz	60 ml	¼ cup
4 fl oz	120 ml	½ cup
8 fl oz	240 ml	1 cup
16 fl oz	480 ml	1 pint

In British, Australian and often Canadian recipes an imperial pint is 20 fl oz. American recipes use the American pint measurement, which is 16 fl oz.

Index